Reference

FRENCH PAINTING
IN THE XXTH CENTURY

THIS VOLUME EDITED BY ANDRÉ
GLOECKNER WAS FIRST PUBLI-
SHED IN MAY MCMXXXIX BY
THE HYPERION PRESS, PARIS.
COLOUR BLOCKS ENGRAVED BY
ETABLISSEMENTS PERENCHIO,
TEXT AND COLOUR PLATES
PRINTED BY IMPRIMERIE DES-
GRANDCHAMPS. PHOTOGRAVURE
BY THEO BRUGIÈRE AND BINDING
BY JOSEPH TAUPIN, PARIS.

FRENCH PAINTING IN THE XXTH CENTURY

BY

CHARLES TERRASSE

Keeper of the Museum of Fontainebleau

Translated from the French by

EVELINE BYAM SHAW

20, J79

THE HYPERION PRESS

LONDON — PARIS — NEW-YORK

MCMXXXIX

THE Painting of the present century, which has not yet run half its course, probably shows stronger, more diverse and more turbulent currents than that of any other. Every form of expression has been attempted, from the direct imitation of the object to the interpretation of the unconscious and the instinctive, and all sorts of techniques and every type of material have been employed. Not only has painting attempted to express by new means what has already been said, but it is continually exploring new paths.

There is no doubt that it would be quite useless to try to find an infallible guiding line to follow through the bewildering chaos of the age. It would be equally useless to attempt to establish, in this summary study, any predetermined order among the mixture of prevailing tendencies. Practically every one of the artists of the present day has belonged to some group which he has eventually left ; and one must remember that their careers are not over.

One may however attempt to sketch the general character of contemporary art, though one must at the same time insist that its diversity is its chief and greatest feature. It must be noted, too, that historians of contemporary art do not agree with each other in the order they give to their studies, and sometimes do not even agree in the classification of individual artists. The best arrangement seems to us to be that adopted by René Huyghe in the " History " published under his direction (*Amour de l'Art* 1933-1934).

Monet said " I paint as a bird sings ", and he meant by that that his picture expressed the joy which his eyes felt in the presence of the beauties of nature, and that he assembled on his canvas his blues, greens and mauves in the same way as a bird " parcels out the measure of its song ". But it is quite otherwise with the painters of the present day. A large number of them have voluntarily submitted their sensibility to fixed rules and are more or less directly guided by theorists. Their art is therefore above all intellectual and dogmatic. For many people, its mysteries must therefore remain a secret, because a full understanding of it can only be attained through study. Each group has its doctrines, or rather, to employ the language of scholasticism, its discipline, confirmed by the practical example and often by the writings of the head of the school.

Seurat was probably the first to proclaim the urgent necessity of dogma, and he and his disciple Signac are the theorists of Divisionism, as Sérusier and Maurice Denis are of Neo-traditionalism. Henri Matisse has been the spokesman of Fauvism, Gleitzes and Metzinger have expounded Cubism, and the apostle of Surrealism is André Breton. Besides this, many artists are also critics, men of letters and lecturers. Odilon Redon was a determined commentator on his own work, and André Lhote is probably the first

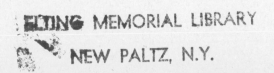

writer on art of the time ; Maurice de Vlaminck is the author of *Dangerous Corner* and Ozenfant and Fernand Léger have published numerous articles.

At its centre each of the groups into which present day artists can be divided is further subdivided, often into irregular fractions. Finally, when a particular member divides himself off too markedly from his original group, he becomes an independent individual ; a fraction becomes a whole number. Masters like Laprade and Derain who were originally grouped under one flamboyant label as " Fauves " have afterwards gone quite different ways.

In general, most contemporary masters have begun under the auspices of Impressionism ; they have then rallied, under the penetrating influence of Cézanne, to the doctrine of Matisse, often with a Cubist phase in between, and have thus finally arrived at a personal expansion of their own.

Diversity and dogmatism are both present ; their resultant, which follows inevitably from such premises, is a characteristic intensity. When logically constructed doctrines are pushed to their furthest extremes, they owe their final form inevitably to the passionate intensity with which they are applied and developed, each in its own special way. The tremendous activity which is going on in art at the present day is by no means all on the surface. Its effects have gone very deep, and every single one of its manifestations and achievements has been the result of reflection and is the consequence or development of first principles.

There is complete freedom of action. Until now the domain of painting was co-extensive with the visible world ; its province was restricted, wide though it was. Form, colour and outline in a picture followed the images of nature. These images were interpreted according to the temperament or the conscious purpose of the artist ; but the things interpreted were real things ; there was no questioning of reality itself. A greater freedom began to appear in Gauguin and Van Gogh ; it applied rather to the colour of the object than to the object itself, though the employment of pure colour, so dear to Van Gogh, already marks a transitional stage.

But as Dufy, I think, has observed, reality is a hypothesis. From among the forms and colours which the eye perceives, an artist will only keep what he intends to keep, and he will omit what he intends to omit ; nature will then seem to him no more than a repertory of things which he can unite or separate, and divide up or reconstruct as he likes. The consequences of this view of looking at things are enormous. The artist may stick to essential which is Fauvism, or he may reconstruct on arbitrary principles in geometric forms which is Cubism, or he may resolve things into their mechanical elements which is Machinism. Moreover, the artist may finally reach the point of no longer taking the outward forms of nature as his guide, but that inner nature which is instinct, the unconscious element which everyone carries within himself. The frequently-quoted saying may be reversed, and whereas one used to say a landscape or a picture was a state of mind, a state of mind may now become a picture ; at this point we have reached Surrealism.

The astonishing spiritual fermentation which we see in the modern schools is the direct consequence of the widespread influence of the great French school of the 19th century and the new liberties which it brought with it.

Perhaps, too, at the root of the matter we may see an aspiration which is a fundamental attribute of human nature — the wish for a life not confined by the water-tight compartments of a social order which has become too sharply divided off into classes.

" Human beings are very often prisoners in some sort of cage ", Van Gogh said. Art is a way of escape.

There have never been so many painters as now ; they can be counted in their thousands. They devote themselves to art with a faith that is almost religious, almost sacerdotal. Neither difficulties nor poverty can stand in their way ; they are in love with beauty, light and liberty, and Gauguin was undoubtedly happier in his hut in Tahiti than when he was a banker and lived in an apartment in Paris. There are many artists who could have led an easy life on the beaten track of official art, with its honorific titles, but who have preferred to stick to their convictions and to risk years of material privation. In fact, there is a spirit of revolt abroad ; revolt against conformity, against accepted ideas of art, against the ready-made, the conventional and the bourgeois. It is remarkable, too, that though perhaps in the days of Impressionism, or of neo-traditionalism, from Monet to Vuillard, artists were mostly of middle-class stock, the " fauves " are, to a large extent, of working-class origin, and are therefore freer.

The contribution from abroad to this flourishing movement is considerable. From all parts of the world people come to Paris, which is its artistic capital ; from Spain, Italy, Germany, Hungary, Bulgaria, Russia, America, the Near and Far East. It will suffice to recall the names of Picasso, Modigliani, Max Ernst, Figari, and Foujita.

Another contribution is that of the Jewish element. Up to the present, no specifically Jewish form of plastic art has been much in evidence. The Jewish race has introduced a quite special vision, an art whose note is one of sadness and mystery. There are, to name no others, Modigliani, Pascin, Soutine, and Chagall. Not being natives of France, they are less attached to ancestral tradition than Frenchmen, and they form an advance-guard of extremists. It is they, too, who, though it is customary to include them in the study of French painting — a custom perhaps less strictly observed now than previously — are more especially grouped under the denomination of the " School of Paris ".

The divergencies between official art, as seen at the Salon, and independent art had become more accentuated during the nineteenth century. The obstructive attitude of the established masters of the Salon gave rise, in 1863, to the " Salon des Refusés ". In 1884, the " Salon des Indépendants " was founded, and the " Salon d'Automne " was to follow in 1903. Cut off from official circles, certain solitary artists devoted themselves to impassioned and profound researches. They were the founders of the modern movement ; Renoir, Cézanne, Gauguin, Van Gogh, Seurat and Redon.

Academic art has been left on one side in the present work. It is an art of honourable traditions, and in the past it showed a considerable power of evolution ; but it has now reached the point of remaining static. The Academic doctrine teaches the theory that beauty cannot come into being without the application of certain fixed and absolute rules which are considered the only true ones. Thus codified, the Academic conception of beauty is doomed to perpetual sameness. It is obvious, when we remember that French art in every sphere, whether that of architecture, sculpture, painting, or engraving, has unceasingly changed and evolved for eight centuries, that a theory, which if it were true would contain the secret of eternal perfection, is futile. It would have been useless therefore to deal here, except by this brief reference, with the existence of Academic art, to which the Salons de la Société Nationale des Beaux-Arts, the Salons des Artistes français, and other bodies bear witness. Excellent and up-to-date examples of it are very rightly given in S. Rocheblave's book *La Peinture française au XIXᵉ siècle*.

We may therefore return to the contemporary movement and its origins in the work of Renoir, Cézanne, Gauguin Van Gogh, Seurat and Redon. For more detailed studies of these artists, the reader is referred to the work of S. Rocheblave, *La Peinture française au XIXᵉ siècle* (French painting in the Nineteenth Century) in the same series as the present work. Here we shall merely recall them briefly to memory.

Renoir is in the purest French tradition. His colour is vibrant and exquisite. Hardly a single artist of the neo-traditionalist group, and even the " Fauves ", has remained un-influenced by him. Under Seurat's influence, the doctrine of divisionism, or neo-impressionism, took shape. Signac and Cross were his pupils. Seurat's researches into static form, which in the *Grande Jatte* for instance, (now in the Metropolitan Museum, New-York), are so sensitive, give him a place among the founders of Cubism. Vincent van Gogh was by birth a Dutchman. His tragic life is a poignant romance. By pure energy, supported financially by his brother who was the earner of a small salary, he formed his style, arriving in Paris in 1886, leaving for the South of France in 1888 and finally becoming insane and committing suicide in 1890. His lyrical feeling, translated into a style of painting remarkable for beautiful tones of almost pure colour, makes him one of the liberators of modern art. " Fauves " and Expressionists to-day alike owe him much. Cézanne, who led a solitary life apart, had a desire for domination. He refused to copy nature, aspired to arrange the landscape before him, and tried to bring it into harmony with his sensibility. His attempt to render form by colour makes him one of the founders of Fauvism. He is also one of the founders of Cubism ; he attempted to restore to Nature the solidity of which the visions of the Impressionists had deprived her, and to do so systematically. " I look for the cylinder ", he said. His obedience to his instincts, in the rendering of form, and his desire to rid those instincts of a dependence on appearances makes him also one of the founders of Expressionism. Through the medium of Gauguin, he was not without influence on the Neo-traditionalist group. There is scarcely a single artist, unless perhaps it is the Douanier Rousseau, who does not owe him something. His *Harlequin* (1888), his *Route du Château Noir* (1896), his *Still Lives* and his *Bathers* contain in essence the whole contemporary movement. Odilon Redon devoted himself for a long time to engraving and lithography before he took to painting once for all. He lived entirely in the sphere of the imagination, cut off from the world. " With the wonders of the visible world before my eyes " he wrote " I have devised an art according to myself alone ". He thought that poetry and strangeness might well have their roots in the mysterious inner regions of the indeterminate where dreams, desires and instincts take their first shape. " Nothing " he wrote again " is done in art by the conscious will alone : everything is done by humble submission to the promptings of the unconscious ". This unconscious world, the world of the indeterminate, was later to become the domain of Surrealism.

NEO-IMPRESSIONISM

Signac, Seurat's disciple, was the spokesman of Neo-impressionism. His book *From Eugène Delacroix to Neo-impressionism*, which appeared in 1899 develops the doctrine of the divisionist school. The object of this doctrine was to put order and reason into the scattered dispersion of Impressionist style. It aimed at the rehabilitation of structure, that is to say of subject. Its technical theory is based on a scientific division of tones. Green, for instance, is a combination of blue and yellow ; to obtain his greens, the artist puts side by side a touch of yellow and a touch of blue and the spectator's eye combines them. Artists who painted in this way were H.-E. Cross, Maximilien Luce, who has rendered both the watery landscape of the Seine valley and also the rough life of the dockyard, Charles Angrand, an extremely delicate colourist, Van Rysselberghe, and a woman of great sensibility, Lucie Cousturier. Aman-Jean, Ernest Laurent, and Le Sidaner came under the influence of this theory, but took it in quite a different spirit.

NEO-TRADITIONALISM

In 1900, Maurice Denis painted a portrait-group, entitled *Homage to Cézanne*. On the easel is set the picture by the Master of Aix, and grouped round it are Odilon Redon, Edouard Vuillard, the critic Mellerio and the dealer Vollard, with Maurice Denis,

Paul Ranson, K.-X. Roussel, and Pierre Bonnard. They form an audience for Paul Sérusier who stands in front of the canvas and comments on it and explains it. The portrait-group is a memorial work of retrospective homage. About 1888, these young painters were all students together at the Académie Julian. It was actually there that Sérusier, who had just come back from a journey to Pont-Aven where he had received the new gospel of Gauguin, communicated this gospel to his disciples. He showed them, in support of his doctrine, a small picture which he had painted at the dictation, so to speak, of Gauguin ; but through Gauguin it was really Cézanne who was the inspiring oracle. Gauguin's words were these : " The inward thought of beings and of things must be revealed, made concrete, and materialised through form and through colours, for it is colour that is the peculiarity of painting. Chiaroscuro and " trompe-l'œil " are unworthy subterfuges. Noble arabesque is alone permissible, that arabesque which leads the feelings through a capricious maze and brings them thus to the heart. In art, all means are good ; nature may be violated and brought, by a sublime deformation, to a permanent beauty ". Again he said : " The stature of the artist is measured by the quality of his transposition ". The essentials of the doctrine were condensed by Maurice Denis as early as 1890 into an often-quoted formula " The chief thing is to remember that a painting..... is a flat surface covered with colours assembled in a certain order ". In reaction against the theory of Impressionism, which made for the breaking-up of form to the point of infinitude in coloured vibrations, this theory allowed for construction and balance of masses, for design, and for wide surfaces of flat colour. The chief thing in fact was to be that the picture was not to be the equivalent of an impression, and in the creation of a picture the eye was not to play a more important part than feeling and reason. It was to be at the same time a rational thing and also a revelation of an enthusiasm or an emotional state. Sérusier, therefore, called his disciples " nabis ", from a term borrowed from the Hebrew, and signifying an enthusiast, one full of faith and ardour. It was a symbolist art, in fact. But that was not all. In their search for a formal equilibrium, the Nabis desired solid ground to set their feet on ; in other words, a tradition. Their admiration for the old masters was to be sufficiently proved by the evolution of their personal genius, and they preferred as a designation the term " neo-traditionalist " rather than " symbolist ".

Thus constituted, the Nabis met throughout a period of several months outside the studio in friendly gatherings at a restaurant in the Brady passage. They then went each his own way. Sérusier eventually returned to Brittany, and painted landscapes, melancholy profiles of girls, and still-life. His rôle as instigator and producer of talent had been considerable. He had revealed to themselves the artists whom we shall now mention.

Maurice Denis, endowed with a keen critical intelligence, and, moreover, a man by the nature of his genius enamoured of breadth and nobility, was first a close follower of Gauguin ; he then devoted himself to the symbolic translation of emotional states in dreamy representations of maidens wandering in parks, and finally took to classic art and mural decoration. Journeys in Italy and the study of the masters of the fourteenth century and of Fra Angelico heightened his aspirations in this direction. A painter of graceful Annunciations and delicate Madonnas, Maurice Denis, as a religious painter, is an heir of the purest traditions. Like the masters he emulates, he expresses himself with most power in vast ecclesiastical decorations. But one finds in his case, as in that of the masters of the Renaissance, no contradiction in the use of themes from the antique for the ornamentation of secular edifices ; examples are the ceiling of the theatre of the Champs-Elysées (1912) and the Cupola of the Petit Palais (1920). However, he is essentially a religious artist. With Georges Desvallières, he is the founder of the Studios of Sacred Art, where, enlisting in his following many artists of deep religious fervour, he is founding, on ancient traditions, a new religious art.

Félix Vallotton is a Swiss by birth but a Frenchman by choice and sympathy. First closely allied to the Nabis, he gradually separated from them. Lucidity and incisive realism are his chief characteristics, taking precedence of colour. He is also a remarkable wood-cutter. Symbolism, dreaminess and the agreeable play of form and colour are absent from his work ; but it has great truth, a direct frankness and a profound honesty. Edouard Vuillard is essentially a painter of intimate themes. His favourite subjects are the dinner-table, dressmaking at a window, reading in a library, people having tea, or sitting in a drawing-room or a boudoir. Sometimes he gives us a street-scene or a view of the sea, but they are seen from the window of a room or from a house. He recurs again to this note of intimacy, which is sometimes simple, but more often at the same time bourgeois and refined, with satiny interiors where the noise of the streets is muffled by carpets and curtains, and a lamp spreads round it the golden inundation of its light. It is perhaps his taste for " conversation pieces " or " figures in a room " that has made Vuillard a portrait-painter without rival.

Vuillard is a harmonist of supreme distinction. For many years he painted small canvasses (or small paste-board panels) in strokes in which tone is shaded into tone. As with Bonnard in his earlier phases, the influence of Japanese prints is clearly perceptible. Greys, browns, greens and blacks are his main colour-schemes ; later his painting became lighter and more vivid in tone. His art is secret and subtle, with a gentle wizardry of charm like that of the purity of a lake or of an aeolian harp. Though in their early day, Bonnard and Vuillard worked in such community of thought and feeling that their art is almost indistinguishable, they evolved ultimately in quite separate directions. Vuillard's nature offered him no inducements to enlarge the secret territory, the walled garden in which it expanded as in a hot-house. Bonnard's nature is of quite another sort, gay, fantastical and ironic but quite without malice, passionately enamoured of life, sensual, and in the highest sense of the word ambitious. This love of life in all its forms is the foundation of the interest he feels in all his surroundings, the countryside, the town, the sea-side, the house he lives in, the fruit and flowers he sees. It is the source of the fascination which animals excercise over him. His world is invariably full of them ; not only does one meet his terrier in his pictures — a dog that has in fact become a legend — but also other dogs belonging to neighbours, besides cats, horses and circus-elephants, which, like Buffon, he delights in because of the careful way they choose their hay. As for the human form, that is vitality itself, and it gives Bonnard the greatest joy every day of his life.

He was first influenced by the Japanese and by Gauguin, and painted in a clear scheme of colour, in dabs and flat areas. Later he renewed contact with the countyside ; he sought examples of reflected light in nature with the heightened effect they give, and abandoning darker tones, he began to use an ascending scale of colour which was further heightened by the bright sunlight of the South of France. Then, with that power of reflection which is one of his characteristics, he again resumed, without losing any of the results of his conquests in the region of pure colour, the study of form. At the present day, he has probably reached the summit of his achievement, and subject with him gives way before ethereal vibrations of colour.

He has always loved Paris and its life, and for many years took part in that life. He often painted Parisian scenes, especially Montmartre — the Boulevard de Clichy, for instance, and the Rues de la Butte. But he also took an interest in the countryside, one might almost say in the earth itself ; and being always fascinated by unknown skies and unfamiliar soil, he has painted Auvergne, Morvan, the Lyons country, and his native Dauphiné. Most of all he has worked in the valley of the Seine from Paris to Vernon, in Normandy, and in the South of France. His portraits, too, are numerous. But his chief interest is in the feminine in its more intimate forms. He is never tired of studying and rendering the beauty of some long thin body with supple movements in the surroundings of the dressing-room. His nudes are pearly and iridescent, and somehow retain, in the settings he gives them, an astonishing purity. These are the aspects of life which Bonnard incessantly renders. In the field of decoration, however, he has produced certain panel-paintings which give evidence of his taste in stylisation and balance of form, always, of course, with a strong imaginative element, for instance the *Monuments* and the *Paradis*, of 1926.

There is nothing in the whole of Bonnard's art which is not young, free and happy. For his art neither suffering nor old age exist ; he has confined himself to contentment. Grace and beauty, scenes of every day life and dreams of loveliness all flourish and expand with him in an exaltation of colour and brilliance which are without equal.

FAUVISM

At the Salon d'Automne of 1905, a new aesthetic appeared of so violent and impetuous a character that it was nicknamed " fauvism ". The word itself, derived from the French word *fauve*, meaning wild, as in the expression " wild beast ", is evidence of what then seemed the unheard-of power and aggressiveness of the movement. Two masters of very different character probably contributed to its origin. One was Cézanne, who had remained for the most part little known and without direct influence on artists in general until the exhibition of his work at the Salon d'Automne in 1904. The other master was Gustave Moreau. It seems very odd that so many artists whose work has nothing in common with his should have been trained in his studio. For an account of Moreau, we refer our readers to the work of S. Rocheblave *La Peinture française au XIXe siècle* (French Painting in the Nineteenth Century) in the same series as the present volume. Moreau's pupils were Matisse, Rouault, Vlaminck, Marquet, and Manguin. Moreau himself was a mixture of two different characters ; the artist, and the man of taste and connoisseur.

It was in his latter character, that of connoisseur, that, with the sensitive liberality of an enthusiast able to appreciate with amazing discrimination the most different types of art, he taught his pupils that art may have a myriad manifestations. What he taught them was not so much a narrow doctrine as the power to look into themselves and to develop their own personalities. " What " he asked " is the importance of Nature in herself ? Nature is merely an opportunity for the artist to express himself. Art is the intense pursuit of the expression of inner feeling through plastic means alone ".

After Moreau's death in 1898, his disciples followed no other masters. They remembered what he had told them, and continued their education in the Museums. It was in Cézanne in the end that they found the basis of a new art.

Fauvism is not a movement which took place of its own accord. During the years between the death of Moreau and its first appearance in a positive form in 1905, it had undergone a process of preparation and ripening.

The principles underlying it are perhaps somewhat as follows. The younger generation of painters wanted to find something new. To that end, they agreed between themselves that it was useless merely to adapt. Construction was necessary, and the field had to be completely cleared and a pure instinct sought for within their own inner selves. Gauguin used to say : " Barbarity is for me a rejuvenation ". The " Fauves " were determined to go back to pure instinct, and they did so. The result was a revolution, and like all revolutions, it had a plebeian character. The Fauves are in fact not of bourgeois origin like the neo-traditionalists, who were content with the social order to which they had adapted themselves, within which, moreover, they were perfectly happy ; the Fauves were mostly of humble origin and had in many cases been engaged in hard manual labour before they were able to live by their art. There was therefore for them no need of compromise ; they made straight for their objective with the energy of instinct. They are, as it were, natural forces. From the plastic point of view, this instinctive vigour is stated by the stylisation of form strongly defined by black outlines and by tones of colour which, by the use of flat areas of pigment, rise to the purest intensity.

This is merely an outline sketch of their general character. Though they share a common point of view on fundamental points, each artist of the group expresses himself according to his temperament. Like the Nabis, like the Cubists in later days, they evolved in different directions.

The Salon d'Automne, where Fauvism first declared itself, owed and still owes its animating force to Georges Desvallières. He too, had been a pupil of Gustave Moreau. His own tendency was towards an art of pathos profoundly rooted in a sincere Catholic faith. For him, as for Rouault, the representation of a courtesan is a showing-up of impurity for what it is ; and he presents the fallen woman in all the degradation of her shame. He has devoted himself to religious art since 1910 and founded with Maurice Denis in 1919 the " Studios of Sacred Art ". At the cemetery of Douaumont he has commemorated the martyrdom of the soldiers of France.

Like his master, Gustave Moreau, he is broad-minded and liberal, and to him is due the honour of having welcomed and protected the new art.

Matisse, painter, draughtsman and sculptor, is also a theorist and the leader of a school. We must give his profession of faith in his own words. " My business is to create an art for people to look at ; for the spectator, to whatever condition of humanity he may belong ; a sort of mental sedative, a sort of pleasurable certaintly, a sort of *truce*, which brings peace and tranquillity ".

The art of Matisse is a static art, economical and concise in the extreme. His subjects are windows opening on the sea, (Salon d'Automne 1905) or a room with half-closed shutters where a woman's form is standing montionless ; and still-lives. His figures and places are of a rather generalised sort as though to absolve the spectator from a too direct interest which might destroy the effect of unity. Nothing could be a better example of the sense of peacefulness he seeks to promote than his picture of *Young Girls in front of the Window* which has a marvellous, dream-inducing quality. In 1905, Matisse made a journey in the South of France and in Corsica. Strong sunlight, which abolishes detail and leaves only essentials, has certainly had no small share in contributing to the artist's sense of those essentials. Matisse works by elimination and allows nothing superfluous to survive. Another influence, in fact a revelation, was Morocco, with its arabesques of brilliant, flat colour. The influence of Morocco is not only seen in some of his subjects, notably the Odalisques, but also in a memory of the typical Mohammedan interior scheme of decoration which appears in his backgrounds, which, while themselves full of movement as designs, contribute, by their emphasis on pure decorative pattern, to the static unity of the picture. After having followed for about twenty years this policy of repose and intimate contact with the spectator he went in 1933 to Oceania, on pilgrimage to Tahiti in honour of Gauguin. In the United States, at Pittsburgh, where he had gone to receive the first prize at the International Exhibition, Dr. Barnes asked him to decorate part of the ceiling of the great hall of his Museum. He painted *The Dance* (1933). It is an example of linear art, without shadows, and shows an extreme economy of means.

The art of Matisse, we may say, then, is absolutely deliberate. It is also a highly-purified, highly selective art. The expression which would best describe it in French is " décanté " — *decanted*. In England, where wine is a luxury, and not as in France a beverage in daily use by all classes, this expression is often supposed to mean simply the pouring of wine from its bottle into an elegant glass decanter suitable for a dining-room table. But in France, where wine is drunk in the kitchen by farmers and peasants, and given, in diluted form, to quite young children, the word " decanted " means, even to the ordinary man, something more, and according to the commonest Dictionary of France, the *Petit Larousse*, to " decant " does not only mean to a Frenchman to pour a liquid, like whisky or gin, from the green bottle in which it is sold into a decanter made of better glass. The dictionary says that it means to transfer into another vessel a liquid which has formed a deposit. Wine, unlike whisky, forms a deposit in the bottle, and to avoid this deposit coming away from the sides of the bottle and getting mixed with the wine, thus spoiling its taste, the wine is very gently poured off into another bottle or " decanter ", in such a way that the deposit is left behind on the sides of the original bottle while the pure wine passes (often through a piece of muslin) into the new bottle. These facts are of course well-known to drinkers of fine old port, Bordeaux, and Burgundy ; but ordinary Englishman may very well not understand how aptly the adjective *decanted* may be applied to the art of Matisse without such explanation. We are not all drinkers of rare vintages, or indeed of wine at all. Matisse's art is rightly described as " decanted " because every superfluity or impurity is carefully kept out of each one of his pictures. Matisse's pictures look roughly and rapidly painted ; but they are in fact most carefully and deliberately thought out, both in colour and in design. There are no dregs in them, no uncertainties, no muddy colour and no muddled form. They are clear, stimulating, and pure like a decanted liquid. Those who disapprove of the use of alcohol may reflect that the stimulation has no bad after-effects ; Matisse does not even wish to intoxicate the eye, let alone the body. Mere prettiness of colour and form has never been his aim. But we may say this of him (and of course the same thing applies to other great artists — one naturally thinks of Bonnard as an obvious example) that to a very peculiar extent a picture by Matisse is like a chemical compound : change one element in it, one colour, one tone, or one line, and the whole meaning of the picture will be lost. There are many admirable pictures of which this is not really true, or not true to nearly the same extent. To admirers of Matisse and Bonnard, as probably most readers of this work already are, this may seem a truism. But reflection will show that it is perhaps truer of Matisse and Bonnard than of many artists, even present-day artists : and this is well illustrated by the extreme difficulty of making the real qualities of these artists' work apparent in reproduction, even in coloured reproduction.

A Braque or a Picasso usually responds far better. Almost any old master can be enjoyed to some extent in a photograph. But certain modern artists' work contains so nicely-adjusted a balance between design, colour, and handling, that a photograph tells one only half or less of what the picture's beauty really consists in. The fact is not insignificant : this is the age of the photograph, the age of the mechanical reproduction of everything, even design and colour. That two of the greatest living artists, not to mention many others, can put something into their work so elusive that it must be sought in the actual picture and in it alone, is perhaps an encouraging sign that there are still essences too subtle to be handled even by the most modern mechanical means.

Dufy first exhibited at the Salon des artistes français in 1901 where he showed his *Fin de journée au Havre* (The end of the day at Havre). He was at that time under the spell of realistic impressionism. His acquaintance with Matisse decided him on a new course. He says himself that he perceived " the miracle of imaginative drawing and imaginative colour ". He gave himself up to the consoling charms of decoration, in the simplest sense of the word, in all its innocence, in its purest, most childlike form. He stylises everything, trees, waves, birds, clouds. Normandy landscapes and sea-sides, racing-scenes, regattas, — the atmosphere of all these is translated by using a sort of shorthand, with the colouring in arbitrary patches. He too, like Matisse, has been touched by the East ; Matisse's Odalisques are represented in his case by Hindu women. The full measure of his decorative genius was revealed in an immense scheme for the Palace of Light which was erected for the 1937 Exhibition in Paris.

Marquet was for a time connected with Matisse — a simple technique, bold lay-out, dark outlines, broad touch. Like Matisse he simplifies, and sticks to the essential. He is extremely absorbed in his subjects and studies them with an intense and quiet interest. Marquet has painted nudes which are admirable in construction and drawing, and landscapes, but it is water which seems to attract him most ; it seems to fascinate him. He used to live on the Quai St. Michel and now lives on the Quai Voltaire. From the windows of his rooms he has the green waters of the Seine and the towers of Notre Dame, massiveness and fluidity embodied, always before his eyes. Marquet has the power of evoking the reflective and thought-producing qualities of water in the most telling strokes and lovely colours. He has looked at it in every phase and climate, in Normandy, Brittany, by the shores of the Atlantic and the Mediterranean, in Norway, and in Egypt, and has expressed the poetic quality which reflection in sea or river water gives to the solid earth and the greenery, the trees, the rocks and the houses that it bears. One is reminded by this enthusiasm for water of the great writer who said " I have always passionately loved water and the sight of it throws me into a delicious dream, though not a dream of anything in particular ". Jean-Jacques Rousseau, to whom we refer, could not have loved water more intensely than Marquet does. In front of one of his wide-spreading sea-scapes one inevitably thinks of the Arab proverb " A man forgets his troubles when he gazes upon the Ocean ". The grandeur, the bigness that the sea confers on everything it touches, men and countries, the grandeur that Stendhal was once so impressed with, reigns supreme in Marquet's pictures.

Othon Friesz, after passing through an Impressionist phase, not to mention an academic one, is another artist who has felt the need to express Nature in terms of his own feelings. His art is one which often attains great decorative breadth, with hardly any emphasis on subject.

Van Dongen is Nordic, and has a romantic nature ; he paints charming flowers. He has become a specialist in the irreverent, even at times malicious representation of his contemporaries, both in male and also more especially in female portraiture.

The satiric and rather perverse side of Van Dongen art has often, too often, distracted attention from his great gifts as a colourist.

Maurice Vlaminck is of Flemish origin and is a profound romantic. He delights therefore in snow-scenes which are often most dramatic, and in moonlit landscapes. His technique reflects his character as a man ; he works feverishly with a lavish use of paint and palette-knife. When one looks at his paintings, one feels that he must experience an actual physical pleasure, the real joy of the artisan, when he has a brush in his hand. He trusts his instinct. " Instinct is at the foundations of all art ", he has said " I try to paint with my heart and my senses without worrying about style ", and like his compatriot Van Gogh, whom he admires, Vlaminck is in fact, as we have said, a furious romanticist.

André Derain, an old friend of his, has an entirely different nature. He has the Latin spirit, the Latin love of order and harmony, and the Latin belief that art must be a matter of considered and conscious creation.

He too has undergone the influence of Van Gogh, as well as of Cézanne. Later he had a " Gothic " phase. (e.g. in his " Last Supper ". (1912-1914). He " found himself " after the war in Italy and especially in Rome. As a landscape and figure-painter, he belongs to the tradition of classic rhythm. His taste for the curious led him to the discovery of Negro Art. The modern passion for the art of the peoples of Africa is due to Derain.

16

Henri Manguin, a disciple of Gustave Moreau, and afterwards a great frequenter of the Museums, was one of the group of Moreau's pupils which included Matisse, Marquet, Rouault, and Camoin. He came to terms with his emotional reactions earlier than Matisse, through the medium of colour. Manguin was already a completely self-possessed artist when he showed his " Hammock " in the " Salon d'Automne " of 1905. Vigorous and delicate nudes, landscapes of the Ile de France and also more especially of the South and its flaming sunshine, ships and the sea and still lives rendered with a remarkable instinct for the actual substance of things which reminds one of Chardin or the Dutch, all these have been painted, with a marvellous eye for the enchantment of colour, by Manguin. Manguin is a man of great native energy and vigour and one sees this in his work ; it has a fiery quality which is the direct reflection of his own flaming conceptions.

Camoin passed through the same stages which went to the making of the other members of the " Fauves " group. He was fired by the same enterprise as Matisse, and went to Morocco with him and Marquet in 1912. But Camoin has an even greater affection for another artist, Renoir. Though in some ways he adheres to the principles of the group in general, for instance in the use of dark outlines, he makes little use of flat areas of colour, and goes in for depth and subtlety. His colour, which is often very brilliant, is a further link with Renoir.

Jean Puy came to Paris from Roanne in 1898, at the age of 22. He was trained at an academy in the Rue de Rennes. He was first an Impressionist, then a Divisionist, and finally found his style through being introduced to the work of Cézanne by Matisse. He aims at truth and simplification. He also aims more directly than Matisse, at life. " Life is what I like best ", he has written " The presence of its gentle pulsations about me is what I love ; I look upon life with a tender eye..... My peculiar difficulty as a painter lies in this very fact, for the relations between tones are barely enough for my purpose ; I should like to express everything, to put life itself into my picture, and that, I know, is an impossibility ".

Henri Lebasque seems to be a sort of connecting link between Matisse and Bonnard ; but he is certainly nearer Bonnard. A representative exhibition lately organised in Paris (Dec. 1938) made it possible to appreciate the merits of his art in all its sensitiveness, harmony, and restraint. Lebasque is not at all an artist of direct statement, in the manner of Matisse, especially the Matisse of before 1910. He neither cares for nor practices the dissonances, the sometimes startling combinations of colour which that master makes use of. He looks not for the exalted, the sublime, but for a winning grace. If Matisse is the painter of the joy of life, Lebasque is the painter of the pleasantness of life.

Close to him, and even nearer to Bonnard, come Albert-André, the decorator Charles Lacoste (who has contributed some cartoons to the Gobelins tapestry-works) and Louis Valtat, who, attracted in turn by Matisse (having been a typical Fauve in 1905) and by Bonnard, is now turning gradually to Neo-impressionism.

On the border-line between two schools, some artists have attempted a combination of the doctrines of Fauvism and Neo-impressionism, a course which brings them appreciably nearer to traditional painting. As in this, subject takes on its old importance, and is taken from life in the case of d'Espagnat and Asselin, from Nature, as with Dufrénoy, and from fiction with Guérin and Laprade.

Dufrénoy has two predilections. First comes his beloved Place des Vosges in Paris, on which the windows of his rooms look out. He is never tired of rendering its peculiar features, its look of a formal garden bounded by high facades with regular fenestration and a gay combination of white stone and pink brick, crowned with roofs tiled with what the Italian architects of the time of Henry IV used to call " azzurrinos ". His other love is Venice. But he paints these traditional subjects with a constructive lay-

17

out and a feeling for the quality of paint in its depths and thickness which give his canvases a particular resonance.

Laprade leans naturally towards an eighteenth-century interpretation of Nature, comprising gardens and foliage as settings for human figures and as a background to Society and Wit in their moments of relaxation. With him as with Dufrénoy the inspiration of his subjects and his technique are opposed to and contrasted with one another, brain and hand working from different angles ; but sometimes they work in combination as in his *Cathedrals*, his *Still Lives*, and above all in his *Flower-pieces*.

Charles Guérin is perhaps the most typical member of this group. He is a true " Fauve ", trained in Moreau's studio. But while he employs the strong vibrating colour typical of the " Fauves ", his subjects are drawn from the classical repertory and from poetic fiction : gardens, arbours, fountains, amorous confidences, parties in park-scenery, pierrots and columbines. Such *fêtes-galantes* were the inspiration of the elegiac lines of poets like Verlaine, Albert Samain, Jules Laforgue, and Théodore de Banville, and Charles Guérin has, as it were, harmonised them in visible form, though the delicate pathos of their poetry is less firmly accentuated, and does not vibrate on so deep a note as the stronger orchestrations of the painter.

Georges d'Espagnat first passed through a stage of loose handling like that of Dufrénoy, but then abandoned " Fauvism " and under the spell of Bonnard sought a gentler, softer and more melting technique. His choice of subject again links him further with Bonnard. He choses by preference interiors and moments of intimate domesticity, and also paints landscape. His women and children are graceful and refined. D'Espagnat is a most delicate portrait painter also, and has done various female subjects and has also painted the poet Paul Valéry, Signac, and Albert-André. He is also a decorator (*Cantegril*, at the Opéra Comique). He makes great play in all his work with dominant tones of strong red.

CUBISM

The present section of this work depends largely upon the passage of René Huyghe's " History of Contemporary Art ", entitled " Introduction to Cubism ", and the quotations are taken from this unless otherwise stated.

" The younger painters are concerned with idealisation, but it is intellectual idealisation, and has nothing to do with the senses. Only the productions of the intellect bear the stamp of immutability, in other words of Truth. Braque's statement, which we shall quote, is a return to the thought of Plato, and the Platonic theory of the transitory character of sense-perception and the permanency of the world of the understanding. It is also related to the thought of Malebranche, the follower of Descartes, which may be summarised in the phrase " Truth does not reside in the senses, but in the intellect. " Braque's statement is as follows. " The senses distort ; the intellect alone is a shaping, a constructive force ". The object of Cubism, therefore, is to substitute for the truth presented to us by our senses that greater reality which belongs to the intellect alone. Realism, the reproduction of appearances as our senses perceive them, is in its decadence, and in its place a new art is to arise which will be a pure mental creation, and entirely abstract. "

The principle of Cubism is already evident in the work of Cézanne, but it has never been possible to give an exact answer to any questions as to who was its inventor, or who disentangled the idea and isolated it. Cubism was really the simultaneous discovery of several artists. About 1907 quite a number of young artists were in search of an art which should prove at once imaginative and constructive. Picasso, Braque and also André Derain were all working at schematic representation about this time. In 1908 the results of these researches were stated with such precision and demonstrative emphasis as to constitute what was practically the manifesto of a new doctrine.

It was at this time that the word " Cubism " made its appearance. Matisse went about saying " Braque's pictures are constructed out of cubes ".

In this first phase of Cubist art natural forms are geometrised, and the design is simple. The facets of the cubes are in places " effaced like crystals whose points and bases have been blackened or smoked. These sudden syntheses of geometrised designs, the so-called " transitions ", are the first and most important discovery of Cubism. The " transition " is the sign, the unrestrained and musical expression of the atmosphere impinging on the forms of objects. Its further significance is that the picture, a conglomerate of indissolubly united objects, is a closed figure composed of open figures ". The above quotation is from André Lhote's " Birth of Cubism " in the above-mentioned " History of Contemporary Art " by René Huyghe.

This " imitative " Cubism was followed in 1910 by " conceptual " Cubism. The outward forms and aspects of things are here abolished ; they are arbitrarily broken up and dissociated, and their fragments become evocative symbols which appeal to and act upon the imagination alone.

Further, Cubism was to attempt to express the fourth dimension, movement, or rather " displacement ". These new researches were inspired by the mathematician Princet, and their aim was the complete and integral representation of the object. Let us again seek counsel of André Lhote. " Princet addresses Braque and Picasso as follows. ' You represent a table as you see it, by the aid of perspective, as a trapeze. But what would happen if you took it into your head to express the Typical Table ? You would have to straighten it out again on your canvas, and turn it into the true rectangular form, instead of making it a trapeze. If the table in the picture is covered with objects which are also distorted by perspective, you will have to straighten those out as well'. The oval representing a glass tumbler will therefore be turned back again into an exact circle. " On this new scheme, Braque and Picasso thought of the idea of making the rectangle of the table like the rectangle of the picture, and arranging the ornamental details of the table on the system of " displacements ". A whole network of lines were therefore set up which enclosed in imaginary cages the different qualities of the things represented, roundness, thickness, transparence, shadows, matt surfaces, grained surfaces, and ornament. When the chosen subject proved refractory to pictorial representation, or when its beauty was such that it would be spoiled by the diminution involved by transposition, the actual thing was *stuck* on to the canvas itself. In this way, one finds pieces of stuff or fabric, whose appearance it was found impossible to imitate satisfactorily, and bits of wall-paper also introduced bodily into the work of these two painters ". This is André Lhote's analysis, taken from Réné Huyghe's above-mentioned work. In practise, what Braque and Picasso were doing was very like what the 17th or 18th century artist was doing when he made what was then called a " quodlibet " or " trompe-l'œil " ; it has never been suggested that they were influenced by these quaint relics of the past, or that their revival of similar devices was a conscious one, but in fact they were dealing, in a more intellectual and fundamental way, with the same problems which our ancestors tackled for the fun of the thing, and as their art progessed, they too seem to have freed themselves more and more from theory, mathematical and artistic, and realised that the only sound reason for doing such things as they were doing was not because they were theoretically " right ", but because they found they *wanted* to do them. They began with conscientious experiment, and ended in pure art — no purer than any other art, but still just as much art for all that. (See " Illustrated London News ". Christmas Number, 1938, for " trompe-l'œils " and " quodlibets ").

However, a considerable group of young artists were practising an art of similar principles, though they avoided pressing these principles to their logical conclusion.

They remained interested in the outside world, in atmosphere, space, and light as we see them. They made their first appearance at the " Salon des Indépendants " of 1911 (in the famous " Room 41 ") and in the " Salon d'Automne ". Their names were Gleizes, Metzinger, Robert Delaunay, La Fresnaye, André Lhote, Fernand Léger, Le Fauconnier, and Marie Laurencin. These are the exponents of *French* Cubism, an art founded on reason, on reflection involved in choice of subject and arrangement, and unlike the purely intellectual Cubism of Picasso in that it allowed an important place to colour. " A constructive and atmospheric art " André Lhote calls it, torn as he is between the rigours of doctrine and the delicious weaknesses of feeling. It is in fact this mystic dualism between theory and feeling which makes the necessary balance between pure plastic values, which are ultimately geometric, and the poetic and mystic values which insinuate their intoxicating essences between the rigid forms of solid objects. The moment was ripe for the application of the theory of " transitions ", and it proved its value by results. Examples are the *Chasseur* by Le Fauconnier, the *Artilleurs* by La Fresnaye, the *Homme au Balcon* by Gleizes, the *Femme en bleu* by Léger, the *Marines* by Metzinger, the *Fenêtres* by Delaunay, and the *Escales* by André Lhote. In these compositions the objects and figures form part of the landscape, losing their thickness and weight, through the medium of the " transition ", in the transparent fluidity of the surrounding air ". Those are the words of André Lhote.

Cubism was the subject of ardent controversies ; it was violently attacked and defended, and extended the field of its conquests. Few contemporary artists have escaped its attractions. Abroad, in Italy, Germany and the Northern countries it had its fanatical adherents. Then came the war. Only the foreign element was left in Paris : Picasso, Juan Gris, Marie Blanchard, Ortiz le Zarate, Zarrage, Severini, William Hayden, and the sculptor Lipchitz.

At this time the direct influence of Picasso began. As André Lhote says " French Cubism, with its smiling aspect and its sensibility was followed by Cubism of an inquisitorial type. Juan Gris tried to put the new artistic ideas on a scientific basis by enlisting in their service the celebrated perspective displacements suggested by Princet, and justifying this application by the aid of the work of physicists and mathematicians like Henry Poincaré and Charles Henry. The application of the expression " fourth dimension " to painting dates from this period, and though it is certainly a wrong use of the term, it served to explain for want of anything better the unreal conception of space induced by displacement ".

At the age of 20, Georges Braque was at the Academie Julian, where he met Friesz, also a native of Havre. He met Picasso and joined forces with him in 1908. Their work together went on uninterrupted till 1914. Their cubist compositions were closely connected. Since the war they have gone separate ways. Braque has remained a Cubist, but he is a French Cubist in the sense indicated above. No artist however has been and remains more true to himself. He paints still-lives and an occasional nude. He is a delicate colourist, whose palette is made up in the main of browns, greens, pinks and greys of wonderfully delicate tones. Lately he has used a lighter scheme running to pale blue and white.

Juan Gris, who comes from Madrid, is a scientific intellectual, who began his training at the School of Arts and Sciences of Madrid, and came to Paris in 1905, and in 1906 met his compatriot Picasso at his studio in the Rue Ravignan. He is an austere theorist, a seeker for the absolute, animated by an invincible faith, and is the purest representative of integral Cubism. Though he would normally have figured in the School of Paris, it seems preferable in the interests of clarity to place him here. The same applies to others (e.g. Van Dongen).

Albert Gleizes and Jean Metzinger were among the first theorists of Cubism. Gleizes follows the line of French Cubism with a tendency to the abstract. He has published notable works on the subject of art.

Metzinger, though always inclined to abstraction, sometimes paints pictures which are realistic in the most readily comprehensible sense. So does Auguste Herbin. Jacques Villon, who began as an engraver, is equally versatile. In his figure-studies he often uses a very carefully-studied technique which has some affinities with divisionism. He is a good colourist.

Georges Valmier comes from Angoulême, and is a particularly gifted decorator. The doctrine of Cubism offers new possibilities for decoration, of a much more attractive character than its possibilities as applied to easel-painting. These artists form a group the organ of which is the review " Abstraction-Création, art non figuratif ", founded by Auguste Herbin. Jean Souverbie again has abandoned Cubism and has entered upon a career as a mural decorator in the most classic sense of the word. In this respect, though formerly nearer to Braque, he is now nearer André Lhote.

DYNAMISM

Fernand Léger began as an architectural draughtsman, and machinery has a fascination for him which he cultivates enthusiastically. After an " essentially Cubist " period from 1910 to 1914, he applied himself, greatly under the influence of his work during the war as a designer of the breech-mechanism of guns, to a mechanical dynamism, the principles of which he extended to the human form. He thus evolved a static and extremely original form of art. He paints in broad areas of brilliant flat colour. With Léger, everything is studied, weighed and analysed ; he leaves nothing to chance. This conscientiousness in the intellectual working-out of a design is accompanied by an equal conscientiousness in execution. Léger is a great artist whose sincerity is absolute.

PURISM

Another doctrine in which the intellect is given supreme status is Purism. Ozenfant is its creator, and Jeanneret is his disciple. Together they have defined their doctrine as follows. " Purism expresses not the variable, or the variation, but the Invariable. A work of art should not be accidental, exceptional, impressionistic, organic, protestant or picturesque, but on the contrary generalised and static ". Purism aims at clarity. It rejects abstraction, but prescribes a choice of subject and arrangement. Eventually Jeanneret separated from Ozenfant, and pursued, under the name of Le Corbusier, an architectural career which is well-known. He later returned to painting.

ORPHISM

Another doctrine which proclaims the undivided sovereignty of pure colour is Orphism, which was given that name by Guillaume Apollinaire. It is a research into the possibilities of colour in the same way that Cubism is a research into those of Form. Cubist pictures are in neutral colours, for colour being a sensuous element is considered inherently inferior. Orphic pictures are violent in colour. Robert Delaunay, the founder of the school, supported by the delicate sensibility of his wife Sonia, has achieved some very curious and attractive results. In order that colours may have their full effect, they must be contrasted ; from this follows the consequence embodied in the word " sim··ltaneousness ". The doctrine leads naturally to a decorative art. The effect produced by Sonia Delaunay in the domain of fashion from 1920 to 1930 was considerable.

CUBIST REALISM

Roger de La Fresnaye.   André Lhote

At the very beginning, when Cubism was in its infancy, about 1908, certain young artists who were enrolled beneath its banner did not entirely accept its creed. They were quite prepared to make use of the new possibilities offered by the theory, at least of the residuum to which they were not antipathetic. But they sought to add to the " plastic metaphors " of linear cubism a more direct, natural and undissociated element. The two most interesting of these young artists from every point of view are Roger de la Fresnaye and André Lhote.

About 1910, La Fresnaye was interpreting nature by means of simplifications very much like those used a little earlier by Braque and Metzinger. But he did not entirely adopt the dogmas of abstraction, and he did not set aside sensibility in the sole pursuit of intellectual activity. In one of his best known pictures, the *Artillerie* of 1912, there is atmosphere and life. The *Conquête de l'Air* is a masterpiece, noble in inspiration and symbolic value. The war had fatal results for de la Fresnaye's exceptional temperament. He received wounds from which he never completely recovered ; despite his natural vigour, he allowed sentimentality to get the better of common-sense, though finally when he was unable to paint anymore, and knew that his death was certain, he expressed his grief in some fine drawings.

André Lhote is very close to him in many ways but is a more positive character. He too refused to succumb entirely to doctrinaire Cubism. Even in the pictures he painted when he was most firmly attached to the Cubist Movement, he shows a taste for the real and for life which sets him apart from pure abstraction. He used the new discoveries with great discernment to express movement as in *Le Rugby*, or space as in the *Natures Mortes* of 1913, or the mirage of the ocean, as in *Escales* (1913). Another cause of his separation from Cubism was his love of colour, for which certain subjects give unrestricted opportunities, and this is the reason of his interest in sailors, ships, motley drapery, and in nature, the landscapes of the South and of Provence. Spain and Venice enchant him for the same reason. Another element in the composition of this many-sided painter is a passion for the Baroque which shows itself in his studio, in a mass of objects of the period of Napoleon the Third, pieces of glass and similar oddments, coloured birds, and negro masks ; and these tastes are reflected in his studio productions and in his direct studies from nature, especially landscape, by a capricious stylisation of form. This baroque element is becoming more accentuated in his work, though he delights also to take a completely different line in some of his nudes which are full of movement and have the effect of Greek goddesses, classical in line, but full of the vigorous life of Ruben's nymphs. The delicately shaded passages which Lhote now seems to use rather more often are seen to excellent advantage in his water-colours. Finally he possesses a critical intelligence of the first order which, seconded by his remarkable literary gifts, makes him the leading writer on art of the present time.

INSTINCTIVE PAINTING

Painters of popular origin and sympathy take a place apart. There is nothing of the doctrinaire about them ; they paint what they like. The laws of drawing, colour and construction in perspective are hardly, if at all, known to them. They rely on instinct for everything. They are chiefly realists.

The greatest of them in all respects is Henri Rousseau, who painted portraits, landscapes and decoration of surprising imaginative force. In his immediate neighbourhood (though these artists are solitary figures and do not form groups) are Bombois, Vivin, and Séraphine Louis, a humble charwoman who does flower pictures almost as she might perform acts of piety.

Maurice Utrillo, the son of Suzanne Valadon, might be included in this section. Instructed by his mother in the rudiments of the art, he paints, as he says of himself, almost as instinctively as he breathes. But there is a certain truth in this whimsical dictum. Though he does not know how he paints, Utrillo is all the same a painter by the very fact of his love of painting. He has a striking power of evoking the leprous atmosphere of the slums of Paris and the streets of Montmartre ; for him there is no hierarchy in art.

Suzanne Valadon may also be placed among instinctive artists. She paints excellent nudes ; and there is also Marie Laurencin, the companion of the " Fauves " and charmingly nick-named " The Fauvette ". There is also Jacqueline Morval who paints flowers, dances, carnivals and bathing-scenes. Hélène Dufau has specialised in decoration and allegory. Hermine David, Hélène Mare, and Geneviève Gallibert have a freer talent. A separate place must be set aside for Louise Hervieu, who with the sole aid of charcoal, has painted magnificently warm and voluptuous symphonies in black and white.

INDEPENDENTS

Neither Cubism with its rather over-emphasised intellectual and linear character, and its rather un-French flavour, nor Fauvism with its excesses, entirely gained the favour of some of the younger generation. Many of them followed their own bent, trusting, like Bonnard, in themselves alone. They may be called the New Independents, and the most important of them is André Dunoyer de Segonzac. Segonzac, who is perfectly familiar with Cubism and Fauvism alike, exhibited as early as 1910 a picture which represented his views as a man of twenty-six, entitled *Buveurs*. Since then in his landscapes, drawings and etchings (he did some striking work inspired by the war) and in his nudes, he has made steady progress along his chosen path. His landscapes are strongly defined and powerfully built. They have a sovereign grandeur, though they are often taken from nature in its simplest form — a road to a village, a road along the side of a hill, a white house, or a little bridge over a stream. There is a bigness about everything Segonzac does, though there may not seem to be any visible means by which the effect is produced. His figures share in this quality, and he has the knack of giving them a mysterious flavour of sensuality. Even his handling of paint contributes to the same effect. Segonzac paints very thickly, as though he seeks a means of self-expression in the actual substance of the pigment. Segonzac's art is in the purest tradition and its vigour and sanity make him one of the leading masters of present-day French Art.

Round Segonzac, though obviously on different planes, may be grouped his close friend Luc-Albert Moreau, Boussinguault, Charles Dufresne, André Marc, Waroquier, and Charlemagne. Moreau and Boussinguault, as well as being splendid painters, are remarkable lithographers. Charles Dufresne, who has painted some quite formal compositions, (*Les Ondines de la Marne*), and some splendid still-lives (*Nature Morte au Torse Antique*), has never forgotten the original revelation, which came to him in Algiers, of the strong light of the South and the East. He leans strongly towards deep and brilliant tone and finds opportunities for it in exotic subjects. Dufresne's colour is excellent.

Henri de Waroquier has been more directly influenced by Cubism. A scientific use of line becomes in his hands a means of expression for a tumult of feeling, and he is essentially a dramatic painter.

Many of these artists have retained not only a love for their native haunts, but some of the main characteristics of their country of origin.

Lucien Mainssieux, with his broad and forceful style, is deeply attached to the beauties of his native Dauphiné. It is the Dauphiné of Bonnard, of Gabriel Fournier, and of Jules Flandrin, with all its beauty of light and all its native luxuriance, that he has chosen to interpret. He has also other predilections. Rome is one of them ; his Roman landscapes are of classic grandeur. There is also the East-Algeria, Tunis, and Morocco.

Georges Bouche hails from Lyons. He is one of the most remarkable of this group. His handling is particularly delicious. There is a mysterious quality in his work ; he expresses, indefinably, the inmost secrets of the city, which are his by right ; he has made them his own.

Then there is Auguste Chabaud. His temperament is one of concentrated passion. His life is wrapt up in the beauty of his native Provence. It is a classic land ; his vision of it is dramatic, because his nature is dramatic, and there is great power in everything he does.

Pierre Girieud and Alfred Lombard are also both Provencal artists. They have made some very interesting experiments in the revival of the art of wall-painting, taking the art of the Quattrocento as their guide. They have done frescoes, with Dufrénoy, in the Chapel of Saint-Pancrace at Pradines, near Grambois (1912). Girieud, in the same spirit, has done some frescoes in the University of Poitiers (1931).

Asselin comes from Orléans and is an " intimist ". The life and work of the home, and scenes of mother love, are his chief inspiration ; but he is also a very sensitive landscape painter. His feeling is fine and reserved and is well seen in his nudes which are constructed with a scrupulousness based on the study of Cézanne.

Alongside of these painters, and like them independent and moderate realists, are Charles Picart le Doux, Vergé-Sarrat, Othon Coubine, Louis Charlot, who works at Saulieu, Kvapil, Savreux, and Jules Zingg.

Paule Jouve, decorator, draughtsman and sculptor, a fervent admirer of the black panther and the royal tiger, is one of the few modern animal-painters. His figures and still-lives have a touch both of Rembrandt and of El Greco.

Maria Blanchard is partly of French and partly of Spanish origin. After a period of whole-hearted Cubism under the influence of Juan Gris, she changed her style and turned to something which is almost realism. Colour plays as important part in her work. Her handling is skilful. The titles of her pictures are themselves significant of her present manner : *Little Girl asleep, Baby's toilet, The Convalescent, The Refugee, The Basket-maker,* and there are also still-lives and figure-studies, carefully thought out and studied work. Her art is essentially human, and in the power of its character-drawing it reaches universality.

Bosshard, who came originally from Switzerland and returned there all too soon, is a painter of landscapes and figures, chiefly the latter, of classic line, precise in manner and of velvety smoothness, and full of that rather intentional simplicity, sometimes almost to the point of coldness, which is typical of Swiss art.

A place apart must be reserved for Foujita. He came to France from the other side of the world ; his themes are those of the West, rendered with the brush of a Japanese. But Foujita has always been more of a draughtsman than a painter ; even of his modelling of the nude, with its fugitive shadows and almost imperceptible relief, this fact remains true. His experiments in religious art — Virgins, Annunciations, Adorations of the Magi, — recall, in twentieth century terms, the firm linear style of the goldsmith-painters of the Quattrocento.

FOREIGN CONTRIBUTIONS

Individuality in whatever form necessarily found the appeal of Fauvism irrestible. It was a revolutionary movement, or perhaps rather a radical movement in the best sense of the word, proclaiming the liberation of instinct and rejecting the bonds of the past and the narrow limits within which art had hitherto been confined. In response to its appeal, many young painters from all over the world flocked to Paris, irrestibly attracted by the new spirit which blazed there in such glory.

They came from Italy, Germany, Hungary, Russia, and the East, and brought with them the natural genius of their own native land. Though their education took shape in Paris, there remained a deep unassimilated element of native origin. These artists from abroad, French by adoption but not actually Frenchmen, formed the school which has been given the name of " l'Ecole de Paris ", " The School of Paris ". Among them are Picasso from Spain, Modigliani from Italy, Max Ernst from Germany, and Soutine from Russia, besides many others.

Many of them and some of the most important, are Jewish or half Jewish. Until recently, there have been no recognised Jewish artists. To the frequent question " Is there really such a thing as Jewish art ", or " Are the Jews really an artistic race " it is now possible to give a positive answer in the affirmative. There is a Jewish style of art, and some of its qualities are entirely outside the boundaries of nationality, and belong to the intrinsic nature of the Jewish people as a race. There is a form of genius which is unmistakably Jewish.

The fundamental characteristics of this genius are an indefinable sadness and remoteness, a special and exceedingly sensitive vagueness. There is an emotional nostalgia in it, the sound as it were of a faint chanting which seems like an echo from times now far distant.

The whole school of painting which represents it has this echo of vague sadness. Neither in subject nor in colour, not even in suggestion, does one find in this school any note of positive joyfulness or gaiety, and in its place there is a melancholy in which the play of intellect takes an abstract form, and becomes a mental activity from which the creative eye of the painter, the eye which creates a harmony of tones by unexplained means, is absent. Numerous Jewish painters have therefore devoted themselves to Cubism, as in the case of Picasso or Marcoussis. It is very difficult to place Picasso. Some of his portraits are drawn with a sureness which reminds one of the precision of Ingres. His more intellectual work, moreover, cannot be fully understood except by the initiated. He has attempted every technique, abandoning each one in turn as he exhausted its possibilities or its interest. But first and foremost, he clearly endeavours to strike fresh notes. He is a passionate and indefatigable researcher and speculator.

Picasso was a precocious child, the son of a drawing-master, born at Malaga, and began painting at twelve years old. Having passed through the Ecole des Beaux Arts at Barcelona, he arrived in Paris in 1900, before he was twenty. One can only note briefly the stages through which his versatile talent has passed. About 1901, he was an Impressionist, then a follower of Van Gogh (Reclining Nude, in the Cogniot collection). From about 1902 till 1905 he was in his " blue period ", from 1905 to 1906 in his " pink period " (both so-called from the dominant colours of his works). The former was of a melancholy cast, often with a suggestion of the theatrical as in the Acrobats and Harlequins. The latter was less severe, almost in fact sweet, as in his " Nudes ". In 1907 there appeared his first essay in voluntary distortion, in the *Demoiselles d'Avignon*. The influence of Polynesian sculpture which Matisse had introduced to him is here evident. In 1908, he was working with Braque, and continued to do so until 1914, at Cubist researches which became more and more abstract. He did, however, devote to Ingres a degree of attention which amounted almost to a cult, in the attempt to attain purity of line. About 1920, Picasso turned his attention to the Antique, distorting his classical figures systematically as though he intended them to symbolise spiritual or intellectual creations. They are strange, enormous, in fact monstrous. Picasso gives evidence of his interest in the monstrous in many scenes in which the bloodthirsty Spanish instinct for cruelty is clearly envisaged, scenes of bull-fighting and the throes of death. But he also draws upon quite other sources and has realised in some of his astonishing Still Lives (Still Life with a Jug, 1931) the static and luminous beauty of stained glass. Then there are also the series of " Formes ", and also his sculpture (1938).

Amédée Modigliani was born at Leghorn. His tragic life ended in Paris in 1920. Italian critics make high claims for him, recognising in him, as also in Spadini and Boccioni " a spirit not only of innovation, but also of profound traditional affinities " ; the phrase is taken from Sig. A. Mairini's " Preface to the Catalogue of the Italian Art Exhibition at the Jeu de Paume ", May 1935. Modigliani's Nudes are his most typical work. With their supple undulating line, they are treated with an economy of means which recalls the art of fresco-painting.

Pascin was born in Bulgaria ; his mother was born in Serbia, but was of Italian origin, and Pascin himself is a naturalised American. He has specialised in the life of the woman of easy virtue. But he has done it as none of his predecessors have, for with him, the woman always partakes to some extent of the child ; Pascin's women seem to hesitate to grow up into adults, and have often the look and carriage of little girls. This side of Pascin's art has a morbid tinge suggestive of adolescent vice, which causes an involuntary shudder. The pictorial style of this artist is in accord with his subjects. His figures have a floating indefiniteness of form which corresponds with the vague backgrounds against which they are seen ; his colours might be called tints rather than pure colours, and he uses grey-whites, misty blues, and black.

Moise Kisling has been influenced chiefly by Derain. In his figure-subjects, and even in his portraits, there is a little of that ambiguous charm and mysterious fascination which is typical of this school as a whole. Chaïm Soutine, who came to Paris from Lithuania in 1911, at the age of seventeen, became associated with Modigliani, but his art has none of the adapted classicism of the latter. Soutine is a Romantic. In his still-lives and his figure-subjects he shows the influence both of Rembrandt and El Greco.

Marc Chagall is one of the most singular and original of all these artists, and shares this distinction with Pascin. In his case, the ancestral character of the Jewish people is combined with a Russian ingenuousness, with a taste for the Bazaars of the East, for brightly-coloured tinsel, vividly painted toys, and popular folk-tales. The strong story-telling instincts of the Jewish race are very marked in Chagall ; his pictures evoke visions of nursery games and villages with gaily-checkered houses inhabited by a population of toyshop characters. Fantasy is heaped upon fantasy ; there are figures flying about in the sky, and animals who talk. His colours are those of a toy box of bricks. Chagall has translated some of the folk-tales of the Jewish peoples of Old Russia, and is connected with the birth of Surrealism.

ONEIRISM AND SURREALISM

The word oneirism, taken from a Greek word meaning a dream, familiar in the English derivatives " oneiromantic " etc., has been invented to describe the strictly mental doctrine of the type of art intended to represent states of mind, the dream-world, and the unconscious, a doctrine which in its eventual manifestations became what is known as Surrealism. The painters who uphold this doctrine are Jean Lurçat, Survage, Salvador Dali, Jean Viollier and Pierre Roy. Lurçat's tendency is towards bare, strongly-defined landscapes suggesting the mountains of the moon, or dynamic creations such as his *Voiles d'Arcachon*, so remarkable for its vivid movement. Sauvage's art is one of construction, and his imaginative gifts are often strikingly evident, as in his *Monte-Carlo* (1916), and his style passes easily into that of broad decorative effect. Various foreign artists belong to the same group, such as Chirico, Campigli, and Tozzi, who are all Italians.

Finally, there is Surrealism, and André Breton is its chief herald. Its nature is at the same time primitive, since instinct and the subconscious are its only motive forces, and also poetic. It might be added that with a few exceptions the painters who have taken part in this movement are not French. André Masson is, it is true, a native of the district of the Oise, but Chirico is an Italian, Joan Miro and Salvador Dali are Spaniards, Hans Arp is an Alsatian, trained at Weimar, Max Ernst and Paul Klee are Germans. The latter is one of the masters of the group.

EXPRESSIONISM

Were it not advisable to avoid, in matters of art, any definitions that are too precise and therefore necessarily narrow and incomplete, one might say of Expressionism that it is the expression of life, but life seen through a personality ; life, that is to say, not in its most detailed or analysed form, but in its most generalised aspect. It is a synthesis, and the synthesis will be all the more powerful in proportion as the artists' personality is powerful. Expressionism gathers individual details into a bunch and generalises from them ; it is an art which aims at reaching the highest point at a bound.

Georges Rouault projects into his work a personality of amazing power. His subjects vary little ; women of the streets, clowns, magistrates, conventional figures like barbarian kings, and finally scenes from the life of Christ. The violence and expressive force of these figures, their aggressiveness, and the convincing universality of their types, is something for which there is no equivalent apart from themselves. The religious side of Rouault's art is unrivalled. He has performed the miracle of giving a new aspect to the sufferings of Christ. Rouault's technique corresponds to the vigorous freedom of his style. Dark blues, strong tones of black, flaming reds, and green, make up his palette. But these colours only tell in flashes : they gleam out among shapes outlined with heavy black strokes. Ronault's pictures have some analogy with stained glass ; and Rouault has in fact practised the craft of the stained glass painter. As draughtsman, painter, lithographer and etcher, Rouault is a master of contemporary satire, and taken for all in all, he is probably the most religious painter, one might say, of the present time.

Henri Le Fauconnier, with his dramatic landscapes, and his symbolical or realistic figures (as in the *Abondance*, or in his *Paysannes zélandaises* of 1914), has had great influence in Scandinavia, Holland and Germany. Amédée de la Patellière, who, like La Fresnaye, died young, was another important artist of this group. Marcel Gromaire is an artist whose synthetic power is amazing, and it has been said of his picture *La Guerre* that it is the most truthful evocation of the War. The means he uses are human guns with wooden heads and hands, clad in steel, cramped in steel, steel of a deep and unforgettable blue, beneath the tragic silhouette of the trench-parapet, waiting : the war was, above all, one feels, an agony of suspense.

The action of his Flemish reaper sharpening his scythe, looking more like a man-machine than a man, caught just at a moment when he has paused for a minute with his hand on his scythe to get his bearings, is something which it would be impossible to find words for ; and *Le Passeur*, with the figure standing in the massive vessel and *La Batelière* also have both alike an unforgettable universality. The same gift for synthesis is seen in his Nudes, in which a delicate and at the same time vigorous appreciation of sensuous qualities is evident. In them Gromaire's evocative powers are strikingly shown ; there is nothing in modern art more powerfully appealing than these figures, usually half-lengths, thrown back with a tremendous agitation of limbs and body, in intense activity. The artist's technique is a very special one ; he paints very thickly, in small touches ; the impasto, both deep and of close texture, appears almost like a vitrified substance. Gromaire is a varied and generous colourist, sometimes extremely delicate, in the grey of winter landscapes or the blond flesh-tones of his nudes, sometimes subdued but glowing as in his Flemish landscape, sometimes startling. Gromaire has something of the Norseman about him and something, too, of the Gothic stained-glass painter.

Goerg's tendencies are similar but like Rouault he is more of a moralist or satirist.

Jean Fautrier and Pierre Bompard must also not be forgotten in this summary.

THE NEW GENERATION

The painters of the most recent generation, Charles Blanc, Legueult, Roland Oudot, and Brianchon, are traditional in manner. They are for the most part delicate colourists, and at present make no secret of their admiration for Matisse and Bonnard ; but whatever their affinities with artists of the past, the future lies with them.

BIBLIOGRAPHY

There is a considerable amount of literature on the subject. A substantial choice has been given here. We may mention that an extremely comprehensive bibliography is contained in *L'Histoire de l'Art Contemporain* edited by René Huyghe.

GENERAL WORKS.

Histoire de l'Art, published under the direction of André MICHEL, vol. VIII, *La peinture française de 1848 à nos jours*, by L. REAU. Paris, 1926.

Nouvelle Histoire Universelle de l'Art, published under the direction of M. AUBERT, vol. II, *L'Art du XXe siècle*, by René HUYGHE. Paris, 1932.

L'Art, des Origines à nos jours, published under the direction of L. DESHAIRS, *L'Art en Europe du XIXe et au XXe siècle*. Paris, 1933.

Histoire Universelle des Arts, published under the direction of L. REAU, *L'Art moderne et contemporain*, by L. REAU.

Histoire de l'Art contemporain, published under the direction of René HUYGHE. Paris, *L'Amour de l'Art*, 1933-1934.

Histoire Générale de l'Art, published under the direction of G. HUISMAN, vol. IV, *L'Art en France au XIXe et au XXe siècle*, by Henri MARTINIE. Paris, 1938.

H. FOCILLON, *La peinture au XIXe et au XXe siècle*. Paris, 1928. — A. BASLER and Ch. KUNSTLER, *La peinture indépendante en France*. Paris, 1929, 2 vols. I. *De Monet à Bonnard* ; II. *De Matisse à Segonzac*. — G. JANNEAU, *Au chevet de l'Art moderne*. Paris, 1923. — P. COURTHION, *Panorama de la peinture contemporaine*. Paris, 1927. — M. RAYNAL, *Anthologie de la peinture française de 1906 à nos jours*. Paris, 1927. — L. HAUTECŒUR, *Réflexions sur la peinture d'aujourd'hui*. Revue de Paris, 1927. *Considérations sur l'art d'aujourd'hui*. Paris, 1929. — H. SEROUYA, *Initiation à la peinture d'aujourd'hui*. Paris, 1931. — Dorette BERTHOUD, *La peinture française d'aujourd'hui*. Paris, 1937. — Raymond ESCHOLIER, *La peinture française au XXe siècle*. Paris, 1937. — J. GORDON, *Modern French Painters*. John Lane, London. — A.-J. EDDY, *Artists and Impressionists*. Chicago, 1919.

PERIODICALS.

Les Arts. — *Gazettte des Beaux-Arts.* — *Beaux-Arts.* — *Revue de l'Art ancien et moderne.* — *L'Amour de l'Art.* — *L'Art Vivant.* — *L'Art d'Aujourd'hui.* — *Art et Décoration.* — *Cahiers d'Art.* — *Bulletin de la Vie Artistique.* — *Le Minotaure.* — *Verve.* — *Burlington Magazine.*

THEORETICAL WORKS AND ARTISTS' WRITINGS.

SIGNAC, *D'Eugène Delacroix au néo-impressionnisme*. Paris, 1911.

VAN GOGH, *Lettres à son frère Théo*. Paris, 1937. *Lettres à Emile Bernard*. Paris, 1911.

M. DENIS, *Théories* (1890-1910). — *Du Symbolisme et de Gauguin vers un nouvel ordre classique*. Paris, 1912. — *Nouvelles théories sur l'art moderne et sur l'art sacré* (1914-1921).

P. SERUSIER, *ABC de la Peinture*. Paris, 1921.

Odilon REDON, *A soi-même* (Journal, 1867-1915). Paris, 1922.

André LHOTE, *La Peinture, le Cœur et l'Esprit*. Paris, 1933. *Parlons peinture*. Paris, 1936.

Henri MATISSE, *Notes d'un peintre*, in *La Grande Revue*, Dec. 25, 1908.

A. GLEIZES and J. METZINGER, *Du cubisme*. Paris, 1912.

Guillaume APOLLINAIRE, *Les peintres artistes, méditations esthétiques*. Paris, 1913.

A. GLEIZES, *Du cubisme et des moyens de le comprendre*. Paris, 1920.

OZENFANT, *Après le cubisme*. Paris, 1920.

A. BRETON, *Le Surréalisme et la Peinture*, in the *Nouvelle Revue Française*, 1926. — *Manifeste du Surréalisme*. Paris, 1929. — *Surrealism and Fantastic Art*, Catalogue of the New-York. Exhibition of Surrealistic Art, 1936.

Les Maîtres populaires de la réalité. Catalogue of the exhibition organised in Paris by the Museum of Grenoble. Paris, 1937.

PRECURSORS OF TWENTIETH CENTURY ART.

A. VOLLARD, *Renoir*, 1920. — G. RIVIERE, *Renoir et ses amis*, Paris, 1921. — ALBERT-ANDRÉ, *Renoir*. Paris, 1928. — Cl. ROGER-MARX, *Renoir*. Paris, 1933. — M. FLORISOONE, *Renoir*. Paris, Hyperion, 1937.

L. COUSTURIER, *Georges Seurat*, in Cahiers d'Art, 1922, 1926. — G. COQUIOT, *Georges Seurat*. Paris, 1934. — André LHOTE, *Georges Seurat*. Paris, 1927. — Cl. ROGER-MARX, *Georges Seurat*. Paris, 1931.

Th. DURET, *Van Gogh*. Paris, 1912. — Ch. TERRASSE, *Van Gogh*. Paris, 1938. — J.-B. de la FAILLE, *Van Gogh*. Paris, Hyperion, 1939.

Ch. MORICE, *Paul Gauguin*. Paris, 1919. — Marcel GUÉRIN. *Œuvre gravé de Gauguin*. Paris, 1927. — R. REY, *Gauguin*. Paris, 1934. — Ch. CHASSE, *Gauguin et le groupe de Pont-Aven*. Paris, 1921. — J. REWALD, *Gauguin*. Paris, 1938. — J. de ROTONCHAMP, *Gauguin*. Paris.

A. VOLLARD, *Cézanne*. Paris, 1915. —, 1919. — G. RIVIERE, *Le Maître Paul Cézanne*. Paris, 1925. — *Paul Cézanne*. Paris, 1933. — Catalogue of the Cézanne Exhibition. Paris, Musée de l'Orangerie, 1936. — P. CÉZANNE, *Correspondance*, edited by John REWALD. Paris, 1937. — J. REWALD, *Cézanne, sa vie, son œuvre, son amitié pour Zola*. Paris, 1939.

A. MELLERIO, *Odilon Redon*. Paris, 1923. — *Odilon Redon* (*Œuvre gravé, Œuvre lithographié*). Paris, 1913.

STUDIES ON INDIVIDUAL ARTISTS (in alphabetical order).

Bonnard, by Fr. FOSCA ; — Ch. TERRASSE. Paris, 1927 ; — Cl. ROGER-MARX.

Braque, by BISSIÈRE. Paris, 1920 ; — M. RAYNAL. Rome, 1921.

Chagall, Ma Vie. Paris, 1931.; — by W. GEORGE (in the " Peintres Nouveaux " series, published by the Nouvelle Revue Française, Paris.)

Coubine, by A.-H. MARTINIE, (" Peintres Nouveaux ", N. R. F.) ; — Ch. KUNSTLER, (" Les Artistes Nouveaux " publ. by Crès, Paris).

Denis, by Fr. FOSCA (" Peintres Nouveaux ") ; — M. BRILLANT, (" Artistes Nouveaux ").

Derain, by Daniel HENRY. Leipzig, 1920 and Amsterdam, 1924 ; — André SALMON, Editions Chroniques du Jour. Paris, 1928 ; — André SALMON, (" Peintres Nouveaux ").

Dufrénoy, by LE MOVREY, (" Artistes Nouveaux ").

Dufy, by Marcelle BERR de TURIQUE. Paris, 1930.

Favory, by E. JALOUX (" Peintres Nouveaux ").

Foujita, by himself in *L'Art d'Aujourd'hui*, 1928 ; — by André SALMON (" Peintres Nouveaux ").

Friesz, by André SALMON, (" Peintres Nouveaux ").

Juan Gris, by Waldemar GEORGE, (" Peintres Nouveaux ") ; — M. RAYNAL, G. STEIN and D. Lord in the Catalogue of the Juan Gris exhibition. Paris, R. Balay and L. Carré, 1938.

Gromaire, by G. PILLEMENT, (" Artistes Nouveaux ") ; — Jean CASSOU, (" Peintres Nouveaux ", 1925.)

Guérin, by KLINGSOR, (" Peintres Nouveaux ").

Kisling, by Florent FELS. Paris, Le Triangle ed. ; — G. GABORY, (" Peintres Nouveaux ").

La Fresnaye, by R. ALLARD, (,, Peintres Nouveaux ").

Laprade, by GEBHARD-CANN. Paris ; — E. JALOUX, (" Peintres Nouveaux ").

Laurencin (Marie), by JOUHANDEAU. Paris, Chroniques du Jour ; — R. ALLARD, (" Peintres Nouveaux ").

Lebasque, by P. VITRY. Paris, 1928.

E. Léger, by E. TÉRIADE, (" *Cahiers d'Art* ") ; — Waldemar GEORGE, (" Peintres Nouveaux ").

Le Fauconnier, by A. SYBAL. Paris ; J. ROMAINS, Amiens.

Léopold-Lévy, by A. SALMON, Le Triangle ed.

Lhote, by P. COURTHION, (" Peintres Nouveaux ", 1926) ; — Madeleine TERRASSE, in *Le Point*, Colmar, 1938.

Lurçat, by Ph. SOUPAULT, in *Cahiers d'Art*.

Mainssieux, by Ch. KUNSTLER, (" Artistes Nouveaux ").

Marchand, by René JEAN, (" Peintres Nouveaux ").

Marquet, by G. BESSON. Paris, 1928 ; — Ch. TERRASSE in *L'Art d'Aujourd'hui*, 1928 ; — Fr. FOSCA, (" Peintres Nouveaux ") ; — M. MERMILLON, (" Artistes Nouveaux ").

Matisse, by M. SEMBAT, (" Peintres Nouveaux ") ; — R. ESCHOLIER. Paris, 1937.

Modigliani, sa vie, ses œuvres ; by A. SALMON, Paris, Chroniques du Jour, 1926 ; — id. ; — A. BASLER, (" Artistes Nouveaux ").

Moreau (L.-A.), by R. ALLARD, (" Peintres Nouveaux ").

Pascin, by CHARENSOL, Paris, Le Triangle ed. ; — G. GOLL, (" Artistes Nouveaux ").

Picasso, by Jean COCTEAU, Paris, 1923 ; *Hommage à Picasso*, in *Documents*, Paris, 1930 ; — Gertrude STEIN. Paris, 1938 ; — REVERDY, (" Peintres Nouveaux ") ; — Henri MAHAUT, (" Artistes Nouveaux ") ; — Jean CASSOU. Paris, 1937.

Rouault, by CHARENSOL. Paris, Chroniques du Jour ; — M. PUY, (" Peintres Nouveaux ").

Rousseau (Henri), by Wilhelm UHDE, Paris, 1911 ; — A. BASLER, (" Peintres Nouveaux ") ; — *Maîtres populaires de la réalité* ; — Catalogue of the Exhibition organized by the Grenoble's Museum. Paris, 1937.

Roussel (K.-X.), by Lucie COUSTURIER. Paris, 1927 ; — L. WERTH, (" Artistes Nouveaux ").

Segonzac (A. Dunoyer de), by P. JAMOT. Paris, 1929 ; — René JEAN, (" Peintres Nouveaux ") ; — Catalogue of the exhibition of his etchings in the Bibliothèque Nationale. Paris, 1937.

Signac, by G. BESSON, (" Artistes Nouveaux ").

Soutine, by Waldemar GEORGE. Paris, Le Triangle ed. ; — Elie FAURE, (" Artistes Nouveaux ")

Utrillo, by M. RAYNAL, in *L'Art d'Aujourd'hui* ; — G. COQUIOT. Paris, 1925 ; — TABARANT. Paris, 1926 ; — A. BASLER, (" Artistes Nouveaux ") ; — Francis CARCO, (" Peintres Nouveaux ").

Valadon (Suzanne), by R. REY, (" Peintres Nouveaux ") ; — A. BASLER (" Artistes Nouveaux ").

Vallotton, by Ch. FEGDAL.

Van Dongen, by Ed. des COURIÈRES. Paris, 1925.

Vlaminck, by Fl. FELS. Paris, 1923 ; — G. DUHAMEL, Paris, " Les Ecrivains Réunis " ; Léon WERTH. Paris, 1925 ; — Francis CARCO, (" Peintres Nouveaux ") ; — André MANTAIGNE, Paris.

THE ARTISTS

ASSELIN, Maurice.
Plate 72.

Born at Orléans, June 1882 ; entered the Atelier Cormon, Paris, 1903. Though at one time a disciple of the Impressionists, Asselin was in the main an independent. He leads a retired life.

BLANCHARD, Maria.
Plate 81.

Born at Santander, 1884 ; father Spanish, mother half French, half Polish. Died in Paris 5th April 1932. Pupil of Van Dongen in Paris (about 1913) ; later teacher of drawing at Salamanca. Returned to Paris in 1916. Became an adherent of thoroughgoing Cubism under the influence of her fellow-countryman Juan Gris, Paris, 1916 ; later severed relations with Cubism. Maria Blanchard, who was afflicted with severe physical deformity, found consolation in religion and in her art.

BONNARD, Pierre.
Colour plate I.
Plates 15, 16, 17, 18, 19.

Born 1867 at Fontenay-aux-Roses, Seine. His father, a native of the Dauphiné, was head of a department in the War Office. His mother was Alsatian. Studied law, but gave up his career as a registrar for painting. At the Academie Julian, he made the acquaitance of Vuillard, Roussel and Serusier, and became a member of the " Nabis " group. His work is varied, and includes portraiture, landscape, decoration, painting, lithography and book-illustration. His palette was at first light in tone, with reminiscences of Japanese Art (1890), then darker, warmer and more glowing : (Parisian life and domestic scenes, 1895-1905). Later it grew lighter again. He was at this time usually away from Paris during the warmer months, at Montval near Marly-le-Roi, then at Vernouillet, Triel, and Vernon. Since 1910 his work has been full of the strong sunlight of the South of France. About 1915 he was aiming at a more compact and constructive use of form, while his colour became even more vibrant and intense. Between 1916

and 1920 he executed the following decorative panels : " Monuments ", " Ville ", " Pastorale " and " Paradis Terrestre " (Earthly Paradise). He is still experimenting in search of new splendours.

BOSSHARD, Rodolph-Theophile.
Plate 82.

Born at Morges, (canton de Vaud) 1889. His father was Swiss (from Zurich) and his mother came from Nîmes, in France. He pursued his studies at the Ecole de Beaux Arts at Geneva.

After travelling in England, Germany and Italy, he worked in Paris. He now lives in Switzerland.

BOUCHE, Georges.
Plate 70.

Born at Lyon, January 1874 ; architectural student at the Ecole des Beaux-Arts-there, where he also got to know the local artist Carrand. Took to painting about 1898 ; exhibited for the first time at the Salon d'Automne and the Salon des Indépendants, 1903.

BRAQUE, Georges.
Colour plate VI.
Plate 44.

Born at Argenteuil, May 1882. Son of a house-painter with artistic leanings. Brought up at Havre where as a young man he got to know Othon Friesz. Came to Paris in 1904 and attended the Academie Julian. He had much in common with Friesz, and their pictures had points of resemblance until 1908, in which year Braque met Picasso, and turned to Cubism, working in close association of ideas with Picasso, but parted company with him after the war. Braque has done decors and theatrical designs for the Russian Ballet.

BRIANCHON, Maurice.
Plate 97.

Born January 1899 at Fresnay-sur-Sarthe, and entered the Ecole des Arts Decoratifs in 1915, where he found much in common with Oudot and Legueult. Paints interiors and landscapes, and has done theatre-decorations.

CAMOIN, Charles.
Plate 30.

Born at Marseille, 1879. Son of an artist-decorator. Entered the École des Beaux-Arts 1896, under Gustave Moreau and there got to know Marquet. On Moreau's death, he left the school, and worked in the Louvre with Marquet. In 1912, he went on a trip to Morocco with Marquet and Matisse. Since the war he spends the winter in Paris as a rule, and the summer at Saint-Tropez.

CÉZANNE, Paul.
Plate 1.

Born and died at Aix-en-Provence (1839-1906). Son of a bank-clerk. Studied at the Louvre, and took part in the Impressionist Exhibition of 1874. Some years later, he left Paris and went to live in his native province, which he scarcely even left except for journeys in Belgium and Holland. His rare work was almost unknown till the Exposition Universelle of 1900. (see S. Rocheblave, *La Peinture française au XIXe siècle* in this series).

CHABAUD, Auguste.
Plate 71.

Born at Nîmes in 1882. In 1901, frequented the Académie Julian and the École des Beaux-Arts (Atelier Cormon).

Soon returned to the South where he led a solitary life at the mas de Martin, at Graveson, a village three or four miles from Avignon.

CHAGALL, Marc.
Plate 84.

Born at Witebsk in Russia, 1887, of poor Jewish parents. Became a painter at the age of twenty ; studied at St. Petersburg, and came to Paris in 1910. Joined the Cubist group which included Gleizes, André Lhote, Delaunay and Apollinaire. During the war, in Russia, he started an art-school at Witebsk (1917) and was compelled to leave it to go to Moscow in 1920, where he worked at stage-decoration for the academic Jewish theatre of Leningrad. Returned to Paris in 1922. He is also an engraver and illustrator.

CHIRICO, Giorgio di.
Plate 86.

Born in 1888 at Volo, (Greece) of Italian parents. Studied at Athens. then at Munich. Lived in Paris from 1911 to 1915, returned to Italy, travelled, and came back permanently to Paris in 1924.

First influenced by Italian art of the Quattrocento (Architectural landscapes) then by the Munich School (Boecklin and Hans von Marees) 1919-1923. Became a Surrealist (1930). Has now returned to representational art. He is also a writer and art-critic.

DELAUNAY, Robert.
Plate 48.

Born Paris 1885. At first an adherent of pointillism, he took to Cubism about 1910. He devoted himself to researches into simultaneous contrasts of colour, christened " Orphism " by Guillaume Apollinaire. Later he studied the expression of speed and movement.

DENIS, Maurice.
Plates 7, 8, 9.

Born Granville (Manche) 1870. Entered Académie Julian then spent some time at the École des Beaux-Arts. Serusier made him a disciple of Gauguin. He quickly became the theorist of the Neo-traditionalist movement. In 1906, with K.-X. Roussel and Émile Bernard, he made a pilgrimage to Aix to see Cezanne. Formal simplification and breadth of design were the inspiration that drew him to monumental painting. He is in fact a powerful decorator. His chief works of this sort are the four great compositions for the Theatre of the Champs Elysées (1912-1913) and the cupola of the Petit Palais (1931). He was deeply religious always, and with Georges Desvallières he founded the Studios of Sacred Art in 1919 : but even before then, his work as a religious painter was considerable. Mural decorations for the church of Vesinet (1901-1903), the chapel of St-Germain-en-Laye (1915-1922), the church of Gagny (1920), the church of the Saint-Esprit, Paris (1935).

Since his early years, he has shown remarkable gifts as a theorist and art critic.

DERAIN, André.
Colour plate IV.
Plates 38, 39.

Born at Chatou 1880. At the age of about fifteen he began to paint and entered Carriere's studio. In 1899 he joined forces with his fellow-countryman Vlaminck, and they worked together. After his period of military service, he worked with Matisse (1905), at Collioure, and exhibited at the Salon d'Automne, 1905 (the so-called " Salon des Fauves "). He showed landscapes of the Collioure neighbourhood. Since 1905, however, he has experimented with constructive stylisation, and despite digressions into archaic manners about 1912, he continues to do so. It was only after the war that he really studied the nude. He has done numerous theatrical decorations, of which one of the best-known in England is the set for the Russian Ballet " La Boutique Fantasque ".

DESVALLIÈRES, Georges.
Plate 20.

Born in Paris 1861. His great-grandfather was Ernest Legouvé. Pupil of Elie Delaunay, then of Tony Robert-Fleury, at the Académie Julian, lastly of Gustave Moreau who was his real master. First exhibited at the Salon des Artistes français ; but since 1886 he took to religious art, and has specialised entirely in it since 1910. As Vice-President of the Salon d'Automne since 1904 he protected original talent of every sort with absolute impartiality. In 1919, he founded the " Studios of Sacred Art " (Ateliers d'Art Sacré) with Maurice Denis and Gabriel Thomas. In 1927 he gave his cartoons for stained glass to the cemetery at Douaumont. With Maurice Denis, he is one of the chief instigators of the rivival of religious art in France.

DUFRENOY, Georges.
Plate 33.

Born at Thiais, 1870. Entered the Académie Julian. Was at first influenced by Impressionism, and since 1902, visits Italy every year. He is a complete independent. He has always lived in the Place des Vosges.

DUFRESNE, Charles.
Plate 64.

Born 1876 at Millemont (Manche), the son of a fisherman. Began as an engraver's apprentice, was then employed by a medallist, and only took to painting at the age of thirty : is self-educated as an artist. After two years in the town of Abd-el-Tif in Algiers (1910-1912) where he discovered the East, he joined forces with Segonzac, Boussinghault and Apollinaire ; found his style about 1920 in allegorical and exotic compositions. Has done theatrical decoration.

DUFY, Raoul.
Colour plate V.
Plates 42, 43.

Born at Havre, 1877. Attended the École des Beaux-Arts at Havre, then joined his compatriot Friesz ; after his arrival in Paris, in 1901, attended the École des Beaux-Arts (Atelier Bonnet). At first influenced by Impressionism his work from 1901 (when he first exhibited at the Salon des Artistes français) till 1908 was close to that of Matisse. He also studied Cezanne. His full originality became evident after the war. By trade a decorator, Dufy remained a decorative artist by choice. He has done

designs for textiles, ceramics and tapestry. He spends his time partly in Paris, partly on the Norman coast, and also at Nice and Cannes. His water-colours are famous, and he has done designs for the cover of " Vogue "

DUNOYER DE SEGONZAC, (André).
Colour plate X.
Plates 60, 61, 62.

Born 1864 at Boussy-Saint-Antoine (Seine-et-Oise) and belongs to the Quercy family. Entered the École des Beaux-Arts 1901 (Atelier of L.-O. Merson). Later pupil of Jean-Paul Laurens at the Académie Julian, then took lessons at the Académie de la Palette. Joined there Albert Moreau and Boussingault. After about four years' work, 1906-1910, his style took shape in the " Buveurs " (1910). During the war, he was a lieutenant in charge of the camouflage section of the Third Army at Noyon, with André Marc, Boussingault, Camoin, Puy and Dufresne as collaborators. From 1920 to 1926 worked at Chaville (Seine-et-Oise) and in the Ile-de-France. Chiefly a landscape-painter. Since 1926 he often visits the South of France (Saint Tropez). Segonzac is also an etcher.

D'ESPAGNAT, Georges.
Plate 32.

Born at Melun 1870, the son of a magistrate. About 1892 became connected with Signac and Cross and later with Bonnard, Vuillard, Laprade and Segonzac.

FAVORY, André.
Plate 66.

Born Paris 1889, nephew of the caricaturist and droughtsman Hermann-Paul. Took to painting at the age of twenty-four. Attended the lectures of Baschet and Royer at the Académie Julian. Became a Cubist roughly between 1912 and 1914, but gradually gave it up. His real masters are the Flemish Painters, especially Rubens. An invalid since 1927, he died in 1936.

FOUJITA (Tsugouharu).
Plate 83.

Born at Edogowa (Tokio), 1886, of noble family. Studied at the Tokyo School of Fine Arts. Trained in the national traditions of his own country, he was already initiated into Western technique and had attained great proficiency in it when he came to Europe in 1912, first visiting London, then Paris. He combines in an entirely personal way the traditions of East and West. He attained great celebrity, spent 1924 in travel, and returned to Japan in 1931.

FRIESZ, Othon.
Plates 40, 41.

Born at Havre, Febr. 1879, of a sea-faring family. After taking lessons with a local artist named Lhuillier, he won a municipal scholarship and came to Paris to attend the École des Beaux-Arts, Atelier Bonnat, where he met Dufy whom he had known as a boy. He became connected with Matisse, Derain, Picasso and especially with Braque. He perfected his technique after the War.

GAUGUIN, Paul.
Plate 2.

Born in Paris 1848 ; died in the Antilles 1903. Part of his childhood was spent with his uncle at Lima, Peru, 1853-1855. Afterwards he lived at Orléans. He left the bank in which he had a comfortable position to devote himself to art about 1880. In 1886 he became friendly with Van Gogh. He settled in Brittany, then went to Martinique, then to Tahiti. From there he returned to Paris in 1893, finaly going back to Tahiti and dying there. (See S. Rocheblave, *La Peinture Française au XIXe siècle*, in this Series).

GLEIZES, Albert.
Plate 46.

Born in Paris Dec. 1881. He was trained by his father who was an industrial designer. He became a Cubist in 1909. While working as an Artist, Gleizes was also a theorist and, in collaboration with Metzinger, has done much writing on art. He has given numerous lectures both in Europe and in America.

GOERG, Edouard.
Plate 45.

Born June 1893 at Sydney, N.S.W., of French parents who settled in Australia. He began painting shortly after arriving in France in 1910. He attended the Académie Ranson where he was a follower of Maurice Denis (1912-1914). Later he was influenced by Daumier and by Rouault.

GRIS, Juan.
Plate 45.

Real Name Jose Gonzales. Born Madrid, March 1887. Died Boulogne-sur-Seine, 1927. His family had intended him for an engineer, but he gave up his career, came to Paris in 1906, at settled at 13, Rue Ravignan (" maison du bateau-lavoir " — a house where many artists have lived who afterwards became famous). Here he formed a close frienship with Picasso. His first paintings date from 1910.

GROMAIRE, Marcel.
Colour plate XII.
Plates 93, 94, 95.

Born in 1892 at Noyelles-sur-Sambre (Nord). While studying law in Paris, he took lessons in Art at the Atelier de la Palette, where he was a pupil of Le Fauconnier. He was called to the colours in 1914, wounded in 1916, and had formed his style as an artist by about 1920. About 1923 he was doing scenes of peasant life (e.g. Le Faucheur Flamand - Flemish Reaper, 1924). Exhibited " La Guerre " at the Independants, 1925. Has done landscapes, nudes, illustration work and etchings. He is a teacher at the Académie Montparnasse, Rue du Départ. He is one of the great masters of Expressionism.

GUÉRIN, Charles.
Plate 35.

Born 1875 at Sens (Yonne). Entered Gustave Moreau's Studio in 1894 ; fellow-student of Matisse, Marquet, Rouault, Manguin. From 1900 onwards, he specialised in " fêtes galantes " which have won him success. Guérin is a notable teacher, and tought at the Atelier de la Palette, rue Val de Grâce, and also at the Académie Moderne, with Friesz, and then at the Académie Clirassi.

JOUVE, Paul.
Plate 73.

Born at Marlotte (Seine-et-Marne) 1882. Pupil of the École des Arts Décoratifs. Jouve has travelled widely, visiting chiefly important towns partly for the sake of their Museums, partly for the sake of their Zoological gardens where he found rare animals as subjects (London, Hamburg, Antwerp, Cairo).

Frequent travels in Africa, the East, and the Far East gave him opportunities for studying wild and fierce animals in their country of origin.

Jouve has also painted landscapes in Turkey, Cambodia and Annam. He is a magnificient decorator.

KISLING, Moïse.
Plate 78.

Born 1891, at Cracow, Poland (then Austrian territory). Son of a tailor. Entered the Cracow Academy in 1906 where he was tought by Josef Pankiewicz, a man of talent, greatly interested in Western European art, and a friend of Bonnard and of Vuillard. This man arranged for Kisling to go to Paris in 1910. He established himself in Montparnasse, and became associated with Braque, Picasso, Juan Gris and Derain. He took part in the War, and became a French subject. The full individuality of his style became evident about 1920.

LA FRESNAYE, Roger de.
Plates 50, 51.

Born at Le Mans, July 1885 ; died at Grasse, Dec. 1925. La Fresnaye was descended from an old Norman family and among his ancestors was Vauquelin de La Fresnaye, a famous poet (16th Century). He entered the Academie Julian in 1903 and became associated with Segonzac, Luc-Albert Moreau, and especially Boussingault. He afterwards frequented the Académie Ranson, where he was taught by Maurice Denis and Serusier. His own style began to form about 1909. He died as a result of having contracted pneumonia during the War. His loss was one of the most serious which contemporary French art has sustained.

LA PATELLIÈRE, Amédée.
Plate 92.

Born 1890 near Mantes ; died in Paris in 1932. After studying at the Ecole Normale, he came to Paris in 1912, and attended the Academie Julian (Atelier Baschet). As with La Fresnaye, he never recovered from the effects of the War. He was three times wounded. He worked in the Vendée district, and in the Ile-de-France.

LAURENCIN, Marie.
Plate 59.

Born Paris 1885. First studied at the Académie Humbert, and first exhibited at the Salon des Indépendants in 1906. She was connected with the group which included Braque, Picasso and Apollinaire, but her style is nevertheless widely separated from Cubism. She is also a decorator (designs for carpets, textiles, and sketches for theatrical decoration).

LAPRADE, Pierre.
Plate 34.

Born at Narbonne 1875 : died December 1931. Trained at Montauban, but formed his own style at the Louvre (1892). Painter and decorator.

LEBASQUE, Henri.
Plate 31.

Born at Champigné (Maine-et-Loire) in 1865. Died in Paris, 1937. Studied first at the Ecole des Beaux-Arts at Angers, and came to Paris in 1886. In spite of a hard struggle to live, he studied under Bonnat at the École des Beaux-Arts. About 1904, he became connected with Rouault, Matisse, and Bonnard. Later he settled in the South of France. He is the author of some fine decorative schemes (Direction des Beaux-Arts, Rue de Valois, Paris ; Hotel Chomard, Transatlantique, Paris ; and cartoons for Aubusson tapestries).

LÉGER, Fernand.
Plate 49.

Born at Argentan in 1881. Was an Architectural draughtsman and retoucher of photographs. Spent two years at the École des Beaux-Arts (1901-1903). Became interested in Cubism in 1908. His taste for mechanics and for scientific research has induced him to bestow on a large number of his works a special flavour of « machinism ». His film « Ballet Mecanique » was an anticipation of the modern films of animated objects.

LHOTE, André.
Plates 52, 53, Colour plate VII.

Born at Bordeaux in 1885 : apprenticed to a sculptor-decorator in wood. Trained at the local school of Fine Arts. Came to Paris in 1907 and thanks to the generosity of an artlover, the deputy attorney-general Granié, spent two years at the Villa Medici free. Became associated in 1911 with the Cubist Group, but never accepted the doctrine in its strictest form, and attempted to reconcile abstraction with nature. He still pursues this method. He is a theorist and teacher, head of an art-school in the Rue d'Odessa, at Montparnasse. Lhote has a considerable influence on contemporary students of art ; he is a subtle and lucid writer and lecturer.

LUCE, Maximilien.
Plate 6.

Born in Paris 1858. Son of a railwayman. Studied at the Ecole des Arts Décoratifs, then became an apprentice to a wood- engraver, and finally entered the Ecole des Beaux-Arts in 1877. In 1884, he went into Carolus Duran's studio. Exhibited for the first time at the Salon des Indépendants, 1887. In 1888, he became an adherent of the divisionist technique, and remained faithful to it for about ten years ; his style came near to that of Impressionism. Affected by extreme left-wing ideas, he was long engaged in the representation of working-class subjects. Since 1917, he has found satisfaction in the landscape of Normandy, and the lower Seine valley, and has rendered its numerous aspects with great feeling (Landscapes of Rolleboise).

LURÇAT, Jean.
Plate 85.

Born at Bruyère (Vosges) in 1892. First studied medicine, then began painting with the decorator Prouvé at Nancy. Came to

Paris in 1910, and became associated with Vildrac and Elie Faure. After the war, travelled all over Europe, and then in America. He is also an illustrator and a decorator.

MAINSSIEUX, Lucien.
Plate 69.

Born at Voiron (Isère) in 1885. Pupil of Flandrin. Studied at the Académie Julian where he became connected with Luc-Albert Moreau and Segonzac. As a landscape-painter, Mainssieux has depicted his native coutryside, but has also felt the attraction of Italy (Rome) and Marocco (Fez, Marrakesh). He is also an etcher, illustrator and has drawn for dramatic criticism. He is an excellent colourist, and has a great curiosity in occult sciences. Mainssieux is an intelligent and avid collector, and has presented his native town with a Museum.

MANGUIN, Henri-Charles.
Plate 29.

Born Paris 1874. Entered Gustave Moreau's studio and became connected with Matisse, Marquet and Camoin. He first exhibited at the Independants in 1902 and took part in the Salon d'Automne, 1905 (Salon des Fauves). In 1907, he travelled in the South of France, discovered St-Tropez, and spent the winters there ever afterwards.

MARCHAND, Jean.
Plate 67.

Born Paris 1883. Pupil of Bonnat and Luc-Olivier Merson at the École des Beaux-Arts. In 1909, he took part in the Cubist movement, but later left the fold, being by predilection inclined to the decorative aspects of art.

MARQUET, Albert.
Colour plate III.
Plates 26, 27, 28.

Born at Bordeaux, 1875. Arrived in Paris 1890. Became a student at the École des Arts Décoratifs, then at the Beaux-Arts in Gustave Moreau's Studio, where he became associated with Matisse. After Moreau's death, he worked with Matisse in the Louvre. In 1902 he exhibited at Berthe Weil's, from 1904 onwards at Druet's. As soon as he could, about 1906, he became an enthusiastic traveller in all parts of the world where there is water, in Europe on the shores of the Mediterranean, in Marocco in 1912 with Matisse and Camoin, in 1920 in Algiers, in 1922 in Tunis, at Sidi Bou Saïd, in 1928 in Egypt. On his return to Paris, he painted the Paris quaysides he has always admired.

MARVAL, Jacqueline.
Plate 38.

Born in October 1866 at Quaix (Isère), died in Paris 1932. Her real name was Marie Vallet. The daughter of a schoolmaster, she was herself for some time an assistant teacher. She became separated from her husband and lived in a small way as a dressmaker at Grenoble. She then began to paint, and afterwards, while living in Paris, was for many years the companion of Jules Flandrin. She exhibited at the Indépendants as early as 1901, and also at the Salon d'Automne. Marval was a decorator (Salon de la Danse, at the Theatre of the Champs Elysées ; designs and drawings for textiles).

MATISSE, Henri.
Colour plate II.
Plates 21, 22, 23, 24, 25.

Born at Chateau-Cambresis (Nord), Dec. 1869. Came to Paris to finish reading for the bar (1890). Entered the École des Beaux-Arts 1893, first in Bouguereau's studio, then in Ferrier's, and lastly in Gustave Moreau's, where he became associated with Rouault, Marquet, Manguin, and Camoin. He trained himself at the Louvre. In 1899, in Carrière's studio, he became associated with Derain, Puy, and Laprage. He pursued his studies with tenacity, trying different techniques. He was well on the way to the realisation of his aims by 1905 (Salon d'Automne) and became completely himself in 1906 (in his painting La Joie de Vivre). His studio, the Couvent des Oiseaux, rue de Sèvres, was frequented by his students, notably the American Bruce and the German Hans M. Purrmann. In 1908, Matisse moved his studio to the Couvent du Sacré Cœur, and expressed his doctrines in "A Painter's notes", published in the Grande Revue, a statement which became the charter of a new phase of Europen Art. In 1911, 1912 he travelled in Marocco. In 1917, settled in Nice. Voyage to Oceania, 1931. In 1933 painted his most important decorative work for Dr Barnes, Marion, USA.

METZINGER, Jean.
Plate 47.

Born at Nantes 1883. Came to Paris at the age of 20. First an Impressionist, then a Divisionist, finally about 1909 became a Cubist. Since about 1920, he alternates between the intellectual game of Cubism and the most direct form of art.

MIRO, Jean.
Plate 87.

Born Barcelona 1893. Student at the Academy of Fine Arts, then the Académie

36

Gali, both at Barcelona. Has been living in Paris since 1919.

MODIGLIANI, Amedeo.
Plate 77.

Born at Leghorn, in 1884, of Jewish parents. His father was a banker. While still very young, in about his fifteenth year, he took to painting, studying at the Academy in Venice and in the Museums. He arrived in Paris in 1906, established himself in Montmartre, and soon experienced extreme poverty. He returned for a few months to Italy in 1909. He then took to sculpture. In 1913 he left Montmartre for Montparnasse. He died exhausted in 1920. His mistress, Jeanne Hébuterne, killed herself on hearing of his death.

MOREAU, Luc-Albert.
Plate 63.

Born Dec. 1882 in Paris. Destined for the law. Attended the Académie Julian where he met Segonzac in Jean-Paul Laurens's studio. He then went on to the Atelier de la Palette. Having been for a time converted to Cubism (till about 1924), he has returned to direct painting. His work in lithography and etching is important.

OUDOT, Roland.
Plate 98.

Born in Paris, July 1897. Studied at the École des Arts Décoratifs from 1912 to 1916, where he met Brianchon and Legueult. A theatre-decorator at first, he then turned more decidedly to painting, (about 1923). He is chiefly a landscape-painter.

PASCIN, Julius.
Plate 79.

Born at Widdin (Bulgaria) in 1885. His father was a Spanish Jew named Pincas, and his mother was Italian, born in Serbia. Finished his studies in Munich about 1900, and came to Paris in 1905. Took part in various publications. Went to America in 1914, and became an American subject. Has travelled for a long time in Florida and Cuba. In 1918, he married Hermine David in New-York, and set up in Paris in 1920, leaving afterwards on further travels. Restless, depressed, and a prey to private anxieties he committed suicide in June 1930.

PICASSO, Pablo.
Plates 74, 75, 76.

Born at Malaga in October 1881. His father came of a Basque family, his mother was a Genoese named Picasso. His father, Ruiz Blasco, was a drawing-master. Picasso was precocious, and was already painting at thirteen. In 1895 he entered the École des Beaux-Arts of Barcelona, and arrived in Paris, aged nineteen, in 1900. From 1900 to 1904, he worked partly in Spain and partly in Paris. Established himself in Montmartre in 1904 in the wooden house at No. 13 Rue Ravignon (now 13 place Émile-Boudeau). This house is the famous " Bateau-lavoir ". Became associated with Max Jacob, Van Dongen, Guillaume Apollinaire, Derain, Braque and Matisse. First Cubist paintings 1906-1907. Left Montmartre for Montparnasse 1912. Did the decor and costumes for Cocteau's ballet " Parade ", music by Erik Satie, in Rome, 1917. It was performed at the Châtelet. Spends his time between Paris and the South of France. Is Director of the Prado Museum.

PLANSON, André.
Plate 99.

Born 1898 at La Ferté-sous-Jouarre (Seine-et-Marne).

Pupil of Meslé, a local landscape painter. Came to Paris in 1921 and studied form a time at the Académie Ranson.

PONCELET, Maurice-Georges.

Born in June 1897 at Mulhausen, he studied under the Polish painter Wielohorsky. Although he has painted landscapes in the Ile-de-France (particularly the Valley of Chevreuse) and the Vendée, as well as interior-pieces (*Nude at the Window* in 1933) and still lifes, he loves above all to exqress the life of the rich, fruitful country (hunting and grape-gathering scenes, *Fête champêtre* of the 1938 Salon d'Automne). His is a bold temperament, inclined towards the solid and the vigorous, and he is enamoured of light wich he knows how to render in very peculiar and often powerful effects.

REDON, Odilon.
Plate 4.

Born April 1840 at Bordeaux : died Paris 1916. Son of a New Orleans colourist who had returned to Medoc, and of a French creole. His family did not oppose his vocation. Intellectual disciple of the botanist Armand Claraud, then of the engraver Rodolphe Bresdin : spent his time between Bordeaux and Paris. Trained himself in the Museums. Decorated a chapel at Arras in 1870. Took to lithography (Dans le Rêve, 1879) and to drawing (exhibitions 1881, 1882) and specialised in it almost entirely till 1900. His art, in which imagination and the dream play so large a part received appreciation from J.-K. Huysmans and E. Hennequin, later from Mallarmé. About 1900, he took to painting again in oils and pastel (portraits, flowers, mythology). Painted decorations in the Château de Domecy at Sermizelles (Yonne) 1900, and at the Abbey of Fontroide (Aude). Gave cartoons for tapestry to the Gobelins manufactory.

ROUAULT, Georges.
Colour plate XI.
Plates 88, 89, 90, 91,

Born at Belleville, 1871, during the Commune. Son of a cabinet-maker of Breton origin, and a Parisian mother. After leaving his primary school, at fourteen he became apprenticed to a stained-glass maker, and attended the evening classes at the École des Arts Décoratifs. He entered Gustave Moreau's studio, and was for five years Moreau's favourite pupil. About 1896, Rouault began to paint landscapes; he renounced the academic style. Then he got interested in travelling theatrical companies, and circuses, street-scenes and street-walkers. He took to pottery making, then to engraving in black and colour for book illustration. He has wrtitten art-criticism, poetry and memoires.

ROUSSEAU, Henri, called " the douanier ", i.e. customs official.
Colour plate VIII.
Plates 55,

Born at Laval in 1844. Died in Paris September 1910. He was a customs official, and was always attracted by painting, to which he devoted himself entirely on his retirement from this position as a minor functionary, in 1886. He was a musician, and writer, and played the violin, the mandolin, and the flute, and wrote ballads. He founded an Academy, called the Polytechnic Association, where he taught painting music and recitation. He exhibited regularly at the Salon des Indépendants from 1886 onwards. He became known to and appreciated by artists like Derain, Vlaminck and Picasso at the end of his life, and also knew the writers Alfred Jarry, Guillaume Apollinaire, Max Jacob, Jules Romains, and Georges Duhamel.

K.-X. ROUSSEL.
Plate 10.

Born at Chêne (commune of Lorry-lès-Metz) in 1867. The son of a doctor, he finished his studies in Paris at the Lycée Condorcet where he got to know Édouard Vuillard, who became his friend and his brother-in-law. At the Académie Julian, he became under the influence of Sérusier, a disciple of Gauguin and was one of the "Nabis" group. But, though occupied with portraits landscapes of Normandy and the Ile-de-France and still-lives, he became increasingly interested in themes from the Antique. His chief work in this line is the

decoration of the curtain at the Theatre of the Champs-Elysées in 1913. He scarcely ever leaves his house (l'Etang-la-Ville) and grows increasingly interested in big decorations.

SEURAT, Georges, 1859-1891.

See the preceding volume in this series. S. Rocheblave, *La Peinture Française au XIXe siècle*.

SIGNAC, Paul.
Plate 5.

Born in Paris, 1863, and died there in 1935. His vocation for art declared itself at an early age, and as soon as he was eighteen, he abandoned the career of an architect, for which his family had destined him, for that of a painter. He was first attracted by the Impressionists, especially so in view of their revolutionary prestige. After this he allied himself with Seurat. In 1884 he became one of the founders of the Salon des Indépendants, ans was elected president in 1908. Signac was almost as much of a sailor as a painter. In 1892, he discovered St-Tropez so celebrated among artists in after years. In 1899, he published his book " From Eugène Delacroix to Neo-Impressionism ", which defined the doctrine of the school. Signac has left us glorious visions of the sea in various aspects from the North Sea to the Black Sea, but most of all of the Atlantic and the Mediterranean. The preliminary water-colours he often makes for his oil-paintings are quite as fine as the finished pictures.

SOUTINE, Chaïm.
Plate 80.

Born at Smilovitchi, province of Minsk, Lithuania, in 1894. Son of a tailor. His childhood was spent in poor circumstances. At twelve years of age he ran away to Vilno, earning his living as a photographer's assistant, while he took lessons in drawing. In Paris, in 1913, he entered the École des Beaux-Arts, Atelier Cormon, and became associated with Modigliani. After Modigliani's death, he lived at Céret (1920-1923), then at Cagnes, and returned eventually to Paris. He lives apart in closely-guarded solitude.

SOUVERBIE, Jean.
Plate 54.

Born Paris 1891. Entered Ecole des Beaux-Arts. Was a disciple of Maurice Denis. Made a lengthy study of the old masters (especially Poussin). He took up Cubism during the years 1924 to 1927, ans has since aimed at a style of Classic tendencies.

38

UTRILLO, Maurice.
Colour plate IX.
Plates 57,

Born December 1883. Son of Suzanne Valadon. He was an illegitimate child, and was recognised, entirely as a matter of courtesy, by the Spanish writer Miguel Utrillo, in 1891. Began to paint about 1903, under his mother's directions. His difficult life was formerly interrupted at intervals by periods in hospital, made necessary by cerebral derangement. He now leads a calm life.

VALADON, Maria-Clémentine, known as Suzanne.
Plate 56.

Born 1867 at Bessines (Haute-Vienne) died in Paris 1937. Came to Paris while still very young, and was a member of a troupe of strolling players, and afterwards acted as model for Lautrec, Puvis de Chavannes, and Renoir. Lautrec encouraged her taste for drawing and painting. She married in 1896, and for the second time in 1909, when she became the wife of the painter André Utter. She had been the mother of a child since 1883, who became the painter Utrillo (see above on Utrillo). She later became associated with Braque, Derain and Picasso, and devoted herself almost exclusively to painting.

VALLOTTON, Félix-Edmond.
Plate 11.

Born at Lausanne in 1865 : died in Paris, December 1925. Arrived in Paris in 1882 and entered the Académie Julian. Contributed drawings and art-criticisms to various periodicals. On the Revue Blanche (Editor Thadée Natanson) he became associated with Bonnard, Vuillard, Roussel, and Cottet. From 1891 to 1897 he devoted himself entirely to wood-cut work, and afterwards never gave up engraving entirely, though he also painted. He also produced several literary works. He is a portrait and landscape painter, but his most important works are his nudes.

VAN DONGEN.
Plate 36.

Born 1877 at Delfshaven near Rotterdam. Son of a sailor. In 1897, after painting a few landscapes and fort-scenes in Holland, he came to Paris and took lodgings in Montmartre, living under conditions of great hardship. Gradually his circumstances improved. He left Montmartre for Montparnasse. He took an interest in every kind of subject, portraits, landscapes, interiors and still-lives, and was perhaps fondest of all of flowers. After the war he became a fashionable artist.

VAN GOGH, Vincent.
Plate 3.

Born at Groot-Zundert, Dutch Brabant, in 1853 ; died at Auvers-sur-Oise, July 1890. Son of a pastor. Began as salesman at Goupil's, then felt the call to a religious life, and finally devoted himself to painting in 1880. Thanks to the generous help, both moral and financial, of his brother Théo who worked at Goupil's and was four years younger, he trained himself, forcing himself to accept his self imposed discipline. Nature was his teacher. In 1885 he spent a few months at the Academy at Antwerp. Reaching Paris in 1886, he attended the Atelier Cormon for a few months, and then went his own way. He became associated with Gauguin, Émile Bernard and Laval. In February 1888 he went to Arles and established himself there. In the light of the South, his palette became resplendent. He cherished the project of founding a communal studio at Arles. In October he was joined by Gauguin. But in December, Van Gogh, then in a low state of health, was seized by a fit of madness. He became an inmate of the Asylum of St-Rémy de Provence, but went on painting. Returning to Paris, in 1890, he established himself at Auvers-sur-Oise, and committed suicide in despair on the 28th of July. His brother only survived him by six months. Van Gogh is a remarkable writer (Letters to Théo, Letters to Émile Bernard).

VLAMINCK, Maurice de.
Plate 37.

Born Paris 1876 : his mother and father were teachers of the piano and violin. His grandfather was Flemish ; his paternal ancestors were Dutch sailors. He was a fine athlete, and at about twenty was a racing bicyclist. He was self-taught as a painter, living on violin lessons : in 1899 he became associated with Derain, then with Matisse. An exhibition of works by Van Gogh (1903) made a great impression on him. Exhibited for the first time in 1905 at the Salon d'Automne, but did not devote himself entirely to painting till 1911. Vlaminck who is not much of a traveller lived for a long time at Chatou, Bougival, and the neighbourhood, and since 1925, at Verneuil-sur-Avre. He is a water-colourist, etcher and potter. As a decorator, he has done cartoons for tapestry.

VUILLARD, Edouard.
Plates 12, 13, 14.

Born at Cuiseaux (Saône-et-Loire) in 1863. After the death of his father, who was a tax-collector, he came with his mother to Paris and settled there. At the Lycée Condorcet, he met K.-X. Roussel, who became his brother-in-law. Entering the Académie Julian he met Sérusier, Bonnard, and Maurice Denis. Vuillard was a member of the "Nabis" group. But his art was always of a very personal nature. It is nearest to that of Bonnard. He is above all an " intimist " and is likely to remain one ; his favourite subjects are interiors, sometimes unassuming, sometimes more luxurious. He is a great portrait-painter. He lives mostly in Paris, spending the winter in Normandy.

WAROQUIER, Henry de.
Plate 65.

Born in Paris, January 1881. Followed Charles Génuys's architectural courses at the Ecole des Arts Décoratifs, and afterwards worked on his own. After feeling the influence of the Impressionists he was attracted by the stylisation of the painters of China and Japan, in addition to that of the Italian Primitives, whom he discovered in 1912, in Italy. He revisited Italy every year till 1931. Then he worked in France (the South, and Burgundy) and in Belgium and Holland.

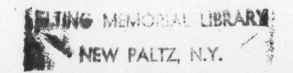
40

PAUL CÉZANNE

THE FRUIT-BOWL (Ca 1877)

Canvas,
Lecomte Collection, Paris.
Photo Vizzavona.

PAUL GAUGUIN

THE LITTLE PIG-KEEPER (1889)

VINCENT VAN GOGH

THE NIGHT-CAFÉ (1888)

ODILON REDON   Photo Druet.
THE RED FLOWER (Ca. 1910)

PAUL SIGNAC   Photo Druet.
THE CHURCH OF NOTRE-DAME DE LA
GARDE, MARSAILLES

MAXIMILIEN LUCE

THE PLASTERER

MAURICE DENIS

"HOMMAGE A CÉZANNE" (1900)

MAURICE DENIS

" SUFFER THE LITTLE CHILDREN TO
COME UNTO ME " (1910)

MAURICE DENIS

THE ORGAN AND THE DANCE (ca 1912)

K.-X. ROUSSEL

BATHERS

Photo Druet.

FELIX VALLOTTON
NUDE STUDY WITH A RED CURTAIN (1921)

Canvas,
Photo Jacques Rodriguez
Henriquez.

11

EDOUARD VUILLARD

PORTRAIT

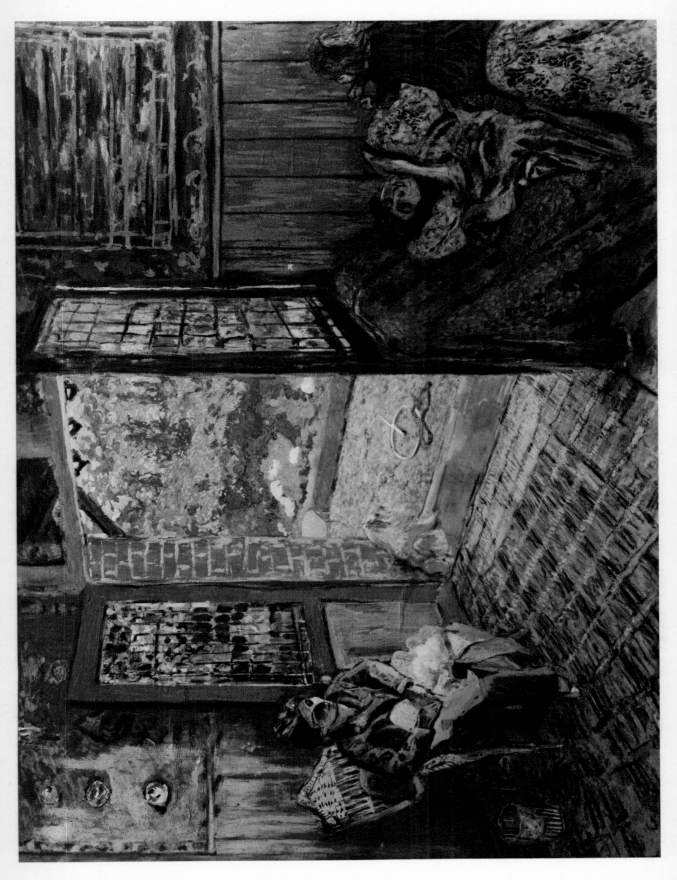

EDOUARD VUILLARD

Photo Jean Gilbert.

SUMMER INTERIOR (1910)

EDOUARD VUILLARD   Photo Druet.

BREAKFAST (CA. 1905)

14

PIERRE BONNARD
LUNCH IN THE OPEN (1902)

Canvas,
Photo Druet.

15

PIERRE BONNARD   Photo Librairie de France.
CHEQUERED BODICE (1892)

PIERRE BONNARD

TORSO (1915)

Canvas,
Photo Bernheim Jeune.

PIERRE BONNARD   Photo Bernheim Jeune.
THE SEINE BANKS AND THE EIFFEL
·   TOWER (ca (1920)

18

PIERRE BONNARD
FLOWERS OF THE FIELD (1914)

19

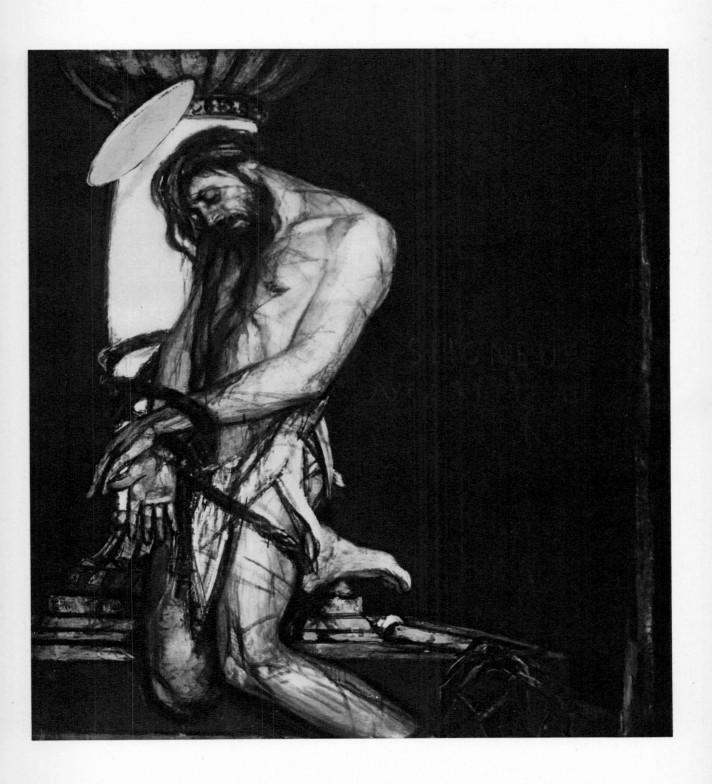

GEORGES DESVALLIERES

CHRIST AT THE COLUMN (ca 1919)

HENRI MATISSE
TWO YOUNG GIRLS AT THE WINDOW

HENRI MATISSE

THE ODALISK WITH MAGNOLIAS (1924)

HENRI MATISSE   Photo Bernheim Jeune.
THE FRUIT-BOWL (1933)

HENRI MATISSE

THE DANCE (1932)

HENRI MATISSE   Decorative Panel. 1938.

Musée du Luxembourg. ALBERT MARQUET Photo Druet.

NUDE STUDY SEATED (CA. 1910)

ALBERT MARQUET   Photo Bernheim Jeune.

THE PORT OF ALGIERS

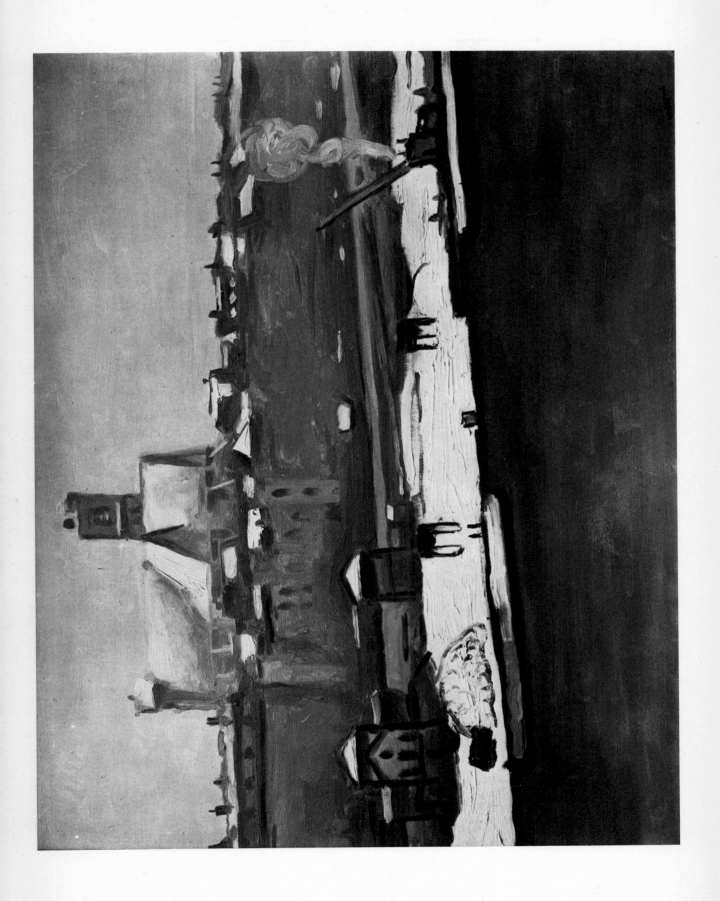

ALBERT MARQUET
THE CHURCH OF SAINT GERVAIS

Canvas,
Photo Bernheim Jeune.

28

Couturat Collection, Paris.   HENRI-CHARLES MANGUIN

THE STUDIO (1938)

CHARLES CAMOIN   Photo Roseman.

PORTRAIT OF LÉON-PAUL FARGUE
(ca 1930)

HENRI LEBASQUE

NUDE STUDY UNDER A TRELLIS (1912)

GEORGES D'ESPAGNAT   Photo Hypérion.
NUDE WOMAN RECLINING ON A COUCH.
(1938)

GEORGES DUFRENOY
VENICE, THE GRAND CANAL (1927)

PIERRE LAPRADE   Photo Druet.
LANDSCAPE

34

CHARLES GUÉRIN

COMPOSITION

Photo Druet.

KEES VAN DONGEN   Photo Marc Vaux.

MISS GRACE LINN (1938)

Galerie de l'Elysée, Paris.　　　　MAURICE DE VLAMINCK

LANDSCAPE

ANDRÉ DERAIN

LANDSCAPE

Canvas,
Photo Librairie de France.

ANDRÉ DERAIN
NUDE STUDY (CA. 1933)

OTHON FRIESZ

VIEW OF THE PORT AT TOULON (1930)

Canvas,
Photo Durand-Ruel.

40

OTHON FRIESZ   Photo Druet.

NUDE FIGURES IN A LANDSCAPE

RAOUL DUFY

NUDE STUDY WITH ARUM LILIES (1929)

RAOUL DUFY

REGATTA ON THE CHANNEL

Photo Druet.

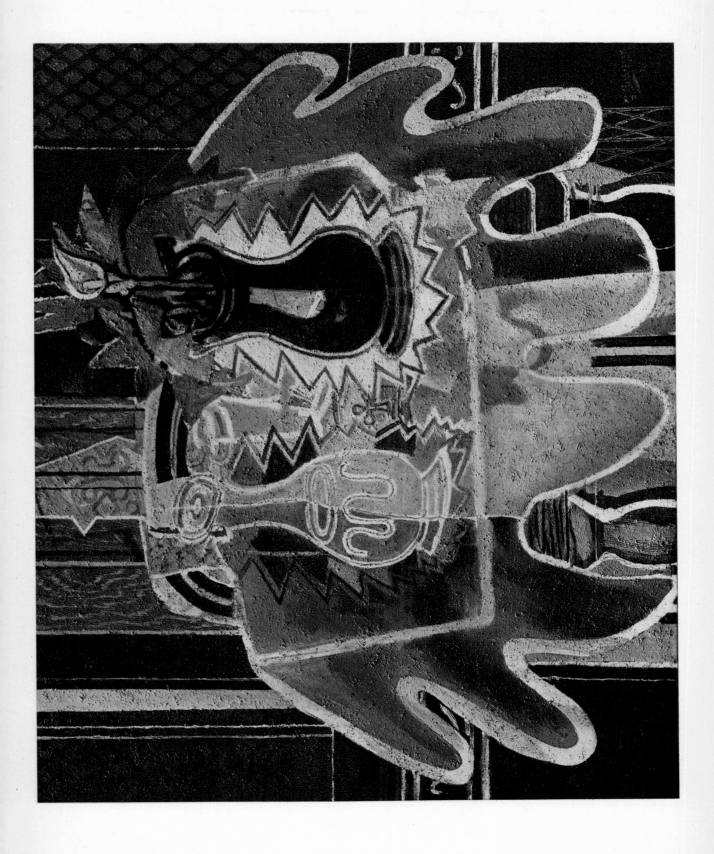

1938.   GEORGES BRAQUE   Canvas.
                                                Photo Paul Rosenberg.
                         STILL LIFE

JUAN GRIS

GERANIUM IN A POT (1915)

45

Léonce Rosenberg Collection   ALBERT GLEIZES   Photo Lemare.

COMPOSITION (1931)

JEAN METZINGER
THE VILLAGE (1921)

ROBERT DELAUNAY

THE EIFFEL TOWER (1911)

Canvas,
Photo Marc Vaux.

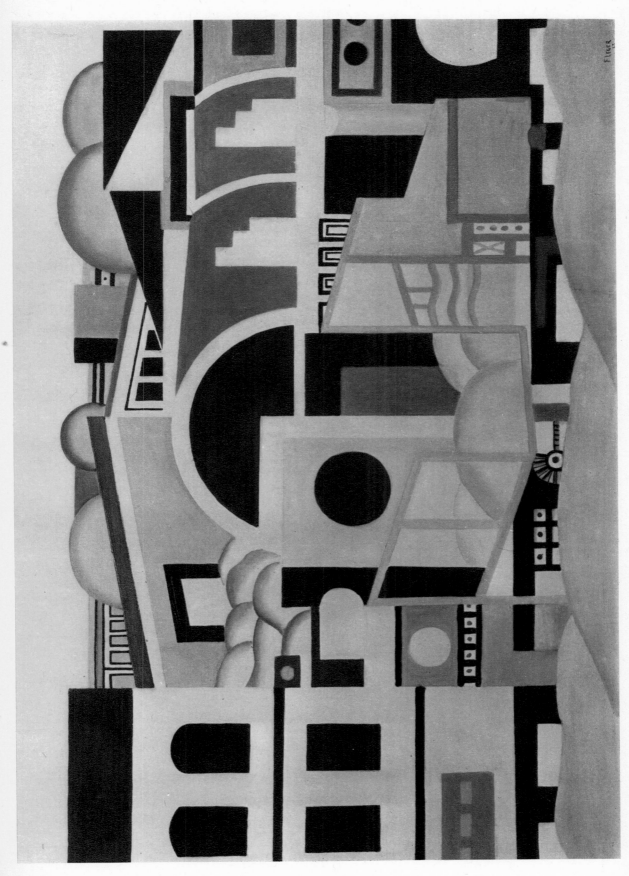

Balaÿ and Carré Collection.   FERNAND LEGER
THE RAILWAY-STATION (1923)

ROGER DE LA FRESNAYE
THE GUNNERS (CA. 1910)

Gaffé Collection, Bruxelles.   ROGER DE LA FRESNAYE
THE CONQUEST OF THE AIR (1913)

51

In the Artist's Collection.　　　ANDRÉ LHOTE　　　Photo Hypérion.
LANDSCAPE (1939)

1939.

ANDRÉ LHOTE

LANDSCAPE COMPOSITION

Canvas,
Photo Marc Vaux.

ANDRÉ LHOTE

HARMONICA-PLAYER

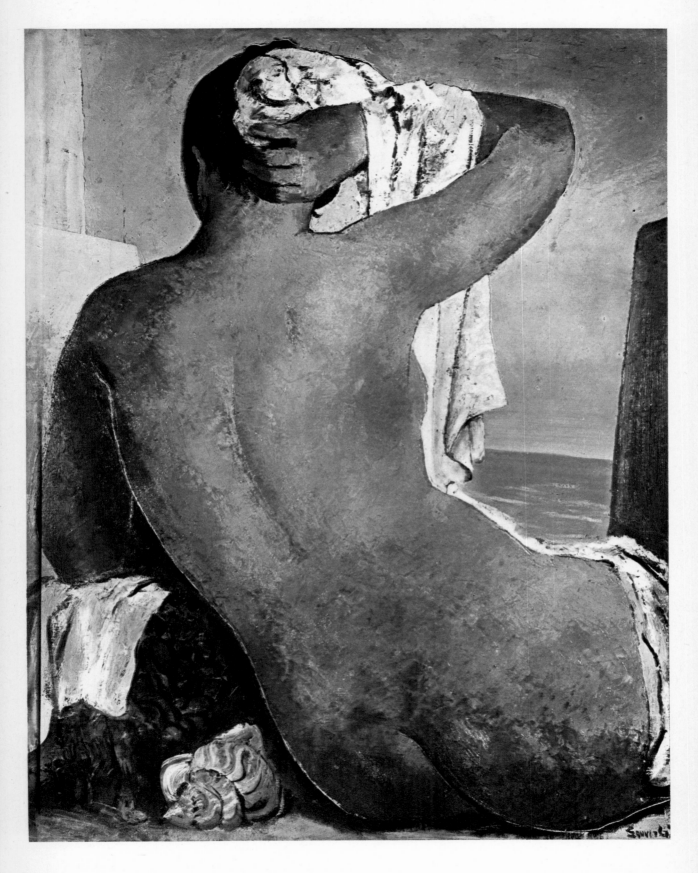

JEAN SOUVERBIE
STUDY OF THE NUDE

Canvas,
Photo Floury.

54

HENRI ROUSSEAU, known as LE DOUANIER   Photo Balaÿ et Carré.

ARTILLERYMEN

SUZANNE VALADON
NUDE STUDY (ca 1920)

56

Gal. Mouradian et Vallotton.　　　　　MAURICE UTRILLO　　　　　Photo Jean Gilbert.

" LE LAPIN AGILE ", MONTMARTRE (1930)

JACQUELINE MARVAL   Photo Druet.
ON THE BEACH (ca 1930)

MARIE LAURENCIN

SYMPHONY (1935)

Canvas,
Photo Paul Rosenberg.

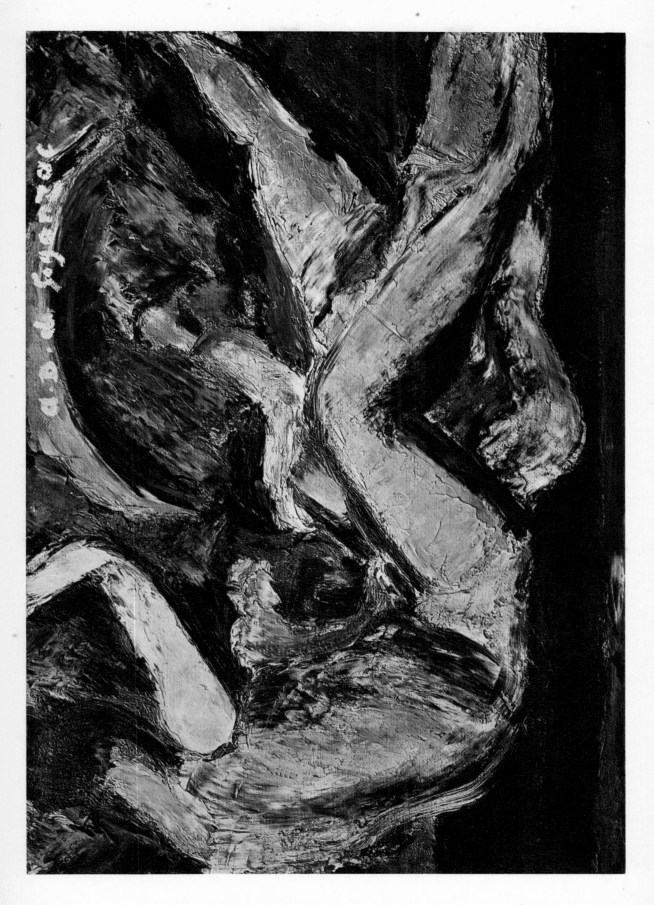

ANDRÉ DUNOYER DE SEGONZAC   Photo Bernheim Jeune.
NUDE STUDY WITH SUNSHADE

ANDRÉ DUNOYER DE SEGONZAC
LANDSCAPE IN PROVENCE (1930)
Collection of Lord Sandwich.

ANDRÉ DUNOYER DE SEGONZAC
STILL-LIFE WITH GLASS OF WINE (1935)

LUC-ALBERT MOREAU
THE EXCENTRIC MUSICIAN

Photo Druet.

Musée du Luxembourg, Paris.　　　CHARLES DUFRESNE　　　Photo Archives Photogra-
　　　　　　　　　　　　　　　　THE PATIO (ca 1935)　　　　　　phiques.

64

HENRY DE WAROQUIER
VIEW OF PERUGIA

Marouteau & Cie.

ANDRÉ FAVORY
THE ARBOUR (ca 1920)

Photo Bernès.

Musée du Luxembourg. JEAN MARCHAND Photo Archives Photographiques.

NUDE STUDY (ca 1920)

MAURICE PONCELET   Photo Marc Vaux.

DONKEY LADEN WITH BIRD-CAGES (1939)

LUCIEN MAINSSIEUX
THE ARCH OF CONSTANTINE IN ROME
(ca 1914)

Photo Morancé.

69

GEORGES BOUCHE

A PEASANT

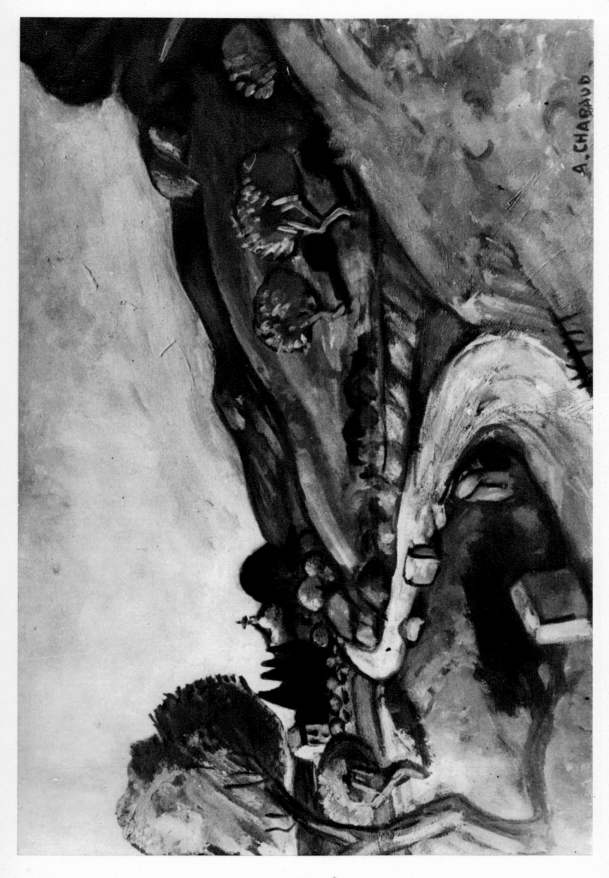

Galerie Katia Granoff.   AUGUSTE CHABAUD   Photo Hypérion,
                          LANDSCAPE IN PROVENCE

MAURICE ASSELIN

THE VILLAGE ROAD

Jean Zay collection.
Photo Hypérion.

PAUL JOUVE　　　　　　Photo Vizzavona.

THE BLACK PANTHER (ca 1938)

PABLO PICASSO   Photo Paul Rosenberg.

TWO NUDE WOMEN (ca 1928)

Collection of Paul Rosenberg

PABLO PICASSO
THREE MUSICIENS (1921)

Photo Paul Rosenberg.

PABLO PICASSO

STILL LIFE (1930)

Canvas,
Photo Paul Rosenberg.

AMEDEO MODIGLIANI
STUDY OF RECLINING NUDE (1917)

MOÏSE KISLING   Photo Bernheim Jeune.

PORTRAIT OF WOMAN IN RED (ca 1930)

Petit Palais, Paris.

JULIUS PASCIN

SALOME (ca 1928)

Photo Bulloz.

Paul Guillaume Collection.

CHAIM SOUTINE

Photo Paul Guillaume.

THE PASTRYCOOK AT CAGNES (1926)

MARC CHAGALL
COMPOSITION (1937)

Photo Marc Vaux.

JEAN LURÇAT

THE FISHERMAN (1935)

Canvas.
Galerie Bucher, Paris.
Photo Floury.

Collection Paul Guillaume.   GIORGIO DI CHIRICO   Photo Lemare.
HORSES ON THE BEACH (Ca. 1928)

Galerie Pierre, Paris.

JOAN MIRO

DUTCH INTERIOR (1912)

Musée du Luxembourg, Paris   GEORGES ROUAULT   Photo Vizzavona.

BATHER (1905)

Ca. 1938.

GEORGES ROUAULT
NUDE STUDY

Photo Marc Vaux.

Ca. 1938.   GEORGES ROUAULT   Photo Marc Vaux.

HEAD OF A CLOWN

Ca. 1931.   GEORGES ROUAULT   Photo Marc Vaux.

                              CHRIST ON THE CROSS

AMÉDÉE DE LA PATELLIÈRE

WOMAN WITH A BOOK